PLAIN FAITH

PLAIN FAITH

A True Story of Tragedy,
Loss, and Leaving the Amish

IRENE & ORA JAY EASH
WITH TRICIA GOYER

ZONDERVAN®

ZONDERVAN

Plain Faith
Copyright © 2014 by Ora Jay Eash and Irene Eash

This title is also available as a Zondervan ebook.
Visit www.zondervan.com/ebooks.

Requests for information should be addressed to:

Zondervan, 3900 Sparks Dr., Grand Rapids, Michigan 49546

ISBN 978-0-310-33683-9

Published in association with the Books & Such Literary Agency, 52 Mission Circle,
Suite 122, PMB 170, Santa Rosa, CA 95409-5370, www.booksandsuch.com.

Cover design: Thinkpen Design
Cover photography: iStockphoto LP
Interior design: Beth Shagene

Printed in the United States of America

To our children and grandchildren.
We are thankful
for your relationships with Jesus Christ,
and that you are diligent to follow Him.
May you have long lives
and may you always have personal relationships
and fellowship with each other.

Contents

Each one should test their own actions.
Then they can take pride in themselves alone,
without comparing themselves to someone else.

GALATIANS 6:4

I will give you a new heart and put a new spirit in you;
I will remove from you your heart of stone
and give you a heart of flesh.

EZEKIEL 36:26

CHAPTER 1

No Simple Choices

ORA JAY

Nothing in life prepares you for losing a child. But losing two daughters on the same night ... the pain is too much to describe. While I was growing up Amish, my life centered on trusting God and believing that His way is perfect; yet I wouldn't be human if I didn't question why a tragedy like this had to happen. And with the questions came guilt ... guilt that I'd been asleep at the road crossing when I should have been awake ... guilt that after having two girls I had worried that I'd never have a son ... guilt that as a father I was supposed to protect my children instead of standing helplessly as they slipped from this world into eternity. Guilt.

What could I do with that guilt except carry it and pretend it wasn't there? At least that's what I believed for many years, that the guilt was mine to carry, that the rules I followed and the life I lived in my community would be good enough to reunite me with my daughters in the afterlife.

Yet as my wife will testify, there was a moment that was even harder than losing the girls. It was the moment we chose no longer to be Amish. The pain of it ripped at our hearts, but on the other side of that pain was hope. Like a rim of sunlight peeking over a storm cloud, the hope was plain and simple — that we could place our salvation in Jesus' hands, not in our works. Could it be enough? Is it enough?

The thought was crazy for those who were raised having the smallest details of their lives and dress under constant inspection. For us Amish — who know the width of each garment's hem, the placement of a prayer *kapp* upon the head, and the correct expression when singing hymns from the *Ausband* — the wild abandon of trusting in grace alone seemed foolish. And walking away from the approval of everyone we knew and loved seemed foolish too.

There are familiar Scripture verses that we learned growing up:

> Come out from among them, and be ye separate, saith the Lord. (2 Corinthians 6:17 KJV)

> Be not conformed to this world: but be ye transformed by the renewing of your mind, that ye may prove what is that good, and acceptable, and perfect, will of God. (Romans 12:2 KJV)

> Be ye not unequally yoked together with unbelievers: for what fellowship hath righteousness with unrighteousness? and what communion hath light with darkness? (2 Corinthians 6:14 KJV)

Yet when Irene and I started reading God's Word for ourselves, we discovered other verses too — like this one:

> Anyone who loves their father or mother more than me is not worthy of me; anyone who loves their son or daughter more than me is not worthy of me. Whoever does not take up their cross and follow me is not worthy of me. Whoever finds their life will lose it, and whoever loses their life for my sake will find it. (Matthew 10:37 – 39)

Plain Faith is the story of how we lost everything — first our daughters, then our community, then our Amish way of life. Some of our old friends claim we left the Amish for the "world." We believe differently. But you'll see that for yourself as you follow our journey.

In the end, our story isn't about what we lost. It's about what we found ...

Whom we found.

CHAPTER 2

The Girls

ORA JAY

August 27, 1982

Children's laughter met our ears as I pulled up and parked our buggy in front of my cousin Floyd's house. Floyd and Ruth lived quite a spell from us, but it was worth the trip because we had two girls who'd be meeting their cousins for the first time.

Irene and the children climbed out of the buggy, and I proceeded to the barn to unhitch the tired horse. After months of good intentions we were finally getting together. All us cousins had been busy with the task of raising our young families. We had long told each other we wanted to get together. We wanted our children to know their cousins. Even though it would be a long night (twelve miles by buggy each way takes nearly an hour and a half), the ice cream social was our first attempt at coming together for fellowship as a family.

My bones were weary as I unhitched the horse, but I tried to hide my tiredness behind a smile. Irene and I had finished building our new house, and I was in the middle of remodeling the barn. Construction occupied my mind and time. If Amish men learn anything, it's a good work ethic. As long as the sun is in the sky, there is work to be done.

Our two daughters, Suetta and Sarah Mae, raced toward their girl cousins. Dark-haired Sarah Mae was always able to keep up with her older sister. She'd learned to walk at nine months old and had never slowed down since. At seven and five, our girls were opposites in so many ways. Suetta was blond with blue eyes and Sarah Mae dark. Irene's family is made up of girls, and when we started having children we had two girls right away, though that troubled me. I thought, *Aren't we going to have any boys?* Later, after we lost the girls, I knew I was being selfish.

Our young boys raced off to play too. Marion, our third child and first boy, had coal-black hair. He was nearly four. Eli Ray, who looked very similar to Marion, was just a little more than two, and Irene was heavy with our next child. With two girls and two boys — and another on the way — I was blessed and thankful for the family God had given me.

Earlier that day Suetta had come in to greet me. It was one of her first days at the local Amish parochial school. She had walked home one and a half miles from the one-room schoolhouse.

"Hey, *Dat!*" She paused at the entrance to the barn. Her golden hair glowed in the sun. She waved, and I offered a quick wave back, but I didn't stop to chat.

I said a simple hello to my daughter but not much more. I had to hurry so we could make it to the ice cream social on time. What I hadn't realized was that short conversation with seven-year-old Suetta would be one of our last. The evening would be filled with conversation and laughter with family, but tears would descend with the darkness.

If I could go back, I would have set aside my work and lingered. I would have asked her about her day. I would have been more patient. I would have listened and remembered — always remembered — her voice.

I wish I could remember more about that night at the ice cream social too. Had Suetta's cheeks turned pink as she raced around the yard with the other children? Had Sarah Mae's eyes grown wide at the taste of the ice cream? Did I give the girls a hug as I lifted them into the buggy? I wish I had. Life changes so quickly, and what had been my biggest concern earlier — getting work done on the barn — mattered little compared to the tragedy we would soon face.

IRENE

It was *gut* spending time with family. If we don't make time for that, it doesn't happen. Days are filled with chores and children — both keep an Amish woman occupied. Our four little ones were a joy, but they kept me busy, and soon we'd have number five. With our new home and the barn being built, I had everything I ever imagined growing up.

It was dark when we left to go home. Buggy lights flashed everywhere as we said our good-byes. With handshakes and waves, we made a plan to get together every month, taking turns in our homes. As it turned out, we never got together like that again.

As we got ready to go home, our oldest son, Marion, who usually sat in the back with the girls, said, "Tonight I'm going to sit between you and *Dat.*" With that, we all climbed into the buggy.

"*Gut,*" Suetta called out, "it'll leave more room for us to sleep," and then she lay down next to Sarah Mae on the backseat, which Ora Jay had folded down into a cot. I didn't know that those would be the last words I would ever hear her speak.

The Indiana air held a bit of a chill, and I snuggled the boys around me. It would be good to get the children home and in bed. We also had a busy day the next day. Of course there aren't many days on an Amish farm that aren't busy.

My head tilted back, resting against the seat back, and soon my eyes fluttered shut. My children's soft breathing met my ears, mingling with the sound of buggy wheels and the horse's footfalls as we made our way home.

ORA JAY

The older girls snuggled down in the back of the buggy. Marion sat between Irene and me, with little Eli Ray on Irene's lap. I finished hitching up the horse and climbed in. The silence from the back told me the girls would be sleeping soon. We never intended to fall asleep, but it overtook us at times. Thankfully, the horse knew the way.

For only one part of the ride home was it of utmost importance that I stay awake. It was a stretch of highway that split our country road in two. Sometimes, especially during the day, I had to wait minutes and minutes to cross because the traffic flowed so fast and heavy.

I don't remember falling asleep to the clomp of the horse's hooves, but I remember waking up briefly. We'd gone a ways down the road from my cousin's place. My heavy eyelids lifted, and I peered through the dark night. In the distance, I noticed the stop sign ahead. I told myself I needed to stay awake for the crossing. But the night was quiet. Too quiet.

My stomach felt full of too much ice cream, and the buggy's gentle sway lulled me once more. The snores of the girls in the back brought a smile. I leaned back to rest my head lightly on the back of the seat.

My eyes fluttered shut again …

It was the blare of the horn that startled me first. The horn of a big truck. Loud, close. Then bright, white light. The jolting of the horse. The overwhelming screech of the semi-truck's brakes.

Headlights bore down. My heart leaped to my throat, and I knew it was going to be close. With a shout and a flip of the reins, I urged the horse forward. Not fast enough.

A crash of splintering wood cut into the night. My body hurled forward. My wife cried out. I don't remember hitting the ground or standing to my feet. But there I was, peering through the inky darkness at Irene and our sons. She seemed fine. The boys were *gut* too. Shaken but fine.

The horse darted down the road, dragging the wheels and the shaft. More pieces of the buggy lay splintered at my feet. I turned around to look for the girls.

The girls!

The moonlight wasn't enough to penetrate the night. My knees trembled as I darted up and down the road, and my voice called their names over and over. *"Suetta! Sarah Mae! Suetta! Sarah Mae!"*

My eyes scanned the roadway, scattered with debris from the buggy. I didn't see them. The semi-truck was coming to a stop far, far down the road. I later heard that the driver had gone to make a phone call to get help. The odor of burning brakes filled the air.

I darted across the dim highway toward the ditch, running and calling their names again. *"Suetta! Sarah Mae!"*

A spot of blond hair caught my attention. They were lying by the side of the road. I ran to them. They looked so small, lay so still. Both of them struggled for breath. They gasped. They needed help.

I have to get them to the doctor.

I turned back to the road. Seeing a passing car, I waved my arms.

"Hey, stop, *stop!*" The car slowed but then continued going. First one and then another. I waved my arms again, frantically, but no one stopped.

Stop! My girls! They need help! Stop!

Minutes passed, though it seemed like hours. With all my energy, I ran to the closest business, which was a hatchery. "Call for help!" They said they would.

I ran back to the girls, to check on them. To see.

Both were gone. It was too late.

They were gone.

Another Amish man came by. I stood in shock as my girls lay lifeless in the ditch. Desperate, I did the only thing I knew to do.

"Let us pray," I told him. We bowed our heads and prayed silently. Amish never pray aloud; it would be too prideful. The Lord's Prayer filtered through my thoughts. It was the only prayer that would come to me. Even in my most heartbroken moment, I didn't know how to connect with God. I'd lived my whole life as an Amish man, but the God I lived my life for was distant and hard to approach. And when I needed Him most, I didn't know how to find Him. Didn't know where to take my pain.

I went back to find my wife. The ambulance had come, and she was being cared for. The boys were shaken but fine. Irene drifted in and out of consciousness. How would she ever make it after losing the girls?

IRENE

I knew I was in the back of an ambulance, but why? Marion was crying. I should comfort him, but I couldn't move. Couldn't think.

The first thing I remember was people asking my name. I could hardly function enough to answer. I could hardly understand their questions.

"Irene. Irene, can you hear me?" Was I waking up from a bad dream?

"Irene, do you know where you are? Irene, do you know what happened?" A man's voice filtered through. Or was it two men? They were talking to me. My body ached. My heart ached too, but I didn't understand.

"Irene, the girls are gone." It was Ora Jay's voice breaking through the fog, and I tried to focus on it. Was he here? I looked around. I remembered lying on the road, but nothing else. I remembered leaving the ice cream social, but nothing after that.

"I hear you," I responded. "I understand." Somewhere deep inside I didn't really understand that both our girls were dead. It wasn't making sense. How? Why? How could this be possible?

The ambulance took us to the hospital. When we got there, our parents were waiting. They already knew about the girls. Someone had gone to their homes — since they didn't have a telephone — to let them know. They had come to the hospital with the tragic thought, *finality*. Everything had changed just like that.

When I saw our parents in the waiting room, the truth of what had happened began to sink in. This wasn't a bad dream. The girls were really gone.

Each of us was checked out at the hospital. We were okay, no broken bones. The staff had compassion for us. Everyone cried.

Our parents wept with us too, and their words matched those echoing in my heart. "Oh my, oh my, oh, how sad. It must have been God's will," they said. I'd been trained to believe that to be true, but the words bounced off my hurting heart.

Our parents told us that my girls were in heaven, and I believed that. The Amish believe that the innocent go to heaven without question. Yet even that didn't help as I thought of the days ahead. Darkness loomed, and God was silent.

ORA JAY

None of us had any injuries that kept us in the hospital. When we went back to the house it was late, yet the house was all lit up. It was strange to see it so bright in a dark night because, without electricity, an Amish home rarely has any lights on. Friends had come and lit lanterns to greet us. But still, this brightness streaming from our windows was a reminder that something had gone terribly wrong.

The next few days were a blur, with people coming and going, providing food, and doing our chores. I had no interest in what was going on outside in the world anymore. All the things I had worked for — the farm, the animals — I didn't care about. Our new house had a nice living room, but Irene and I never had taken the time to sit in it and enjoy it — to spend time with our children there. It showed me that the things of the world — the things we deal with every day — are going to pass away, and they won't mean anything when we meet the Lord.

People would say, "Your girls are better off where they are. They are in heaven." The Amish have an expectation, as most Christians do, that when a youngster dies he or she goes to heaven. It was a great comfort knowing that they were no longer facing any pain or suffering.

Over and over people said, "They are in heaven now," but I longed to hear something else. Something was going on inside me, and I needed comfort. I needed peace in my own soul. I knew my daughters were fine, but I was not. My soul was empty. My heart felt as if it had been ripped out of my chest. I felt alone. God seemed so very far away.

For two nights Amish families filed through the house for the viewings. One by one, old, young, mothers with children, and distant neighbors stood in a long line. Each shook our hands, but few offered words. For those who did speak, their words were simple.

"God bless you."

"They are in heaven."

Today, looking back, Irene and I both wish someone would have shared Jesus with us in our broken state. *Ja*, we knew who He was. We knew of His sacrifice on our behalf. But we didn't understand that He is an ever-present hope, that He is interceding for us before the Father, that He could be as real to us in the present as we hoped He would be someday in heaven. We had been taught that He had died for us, but we didn't understand the grace of Jesus Christ and that we needed to invite Him into our hearts personally to receive that grace for forgiveness of our sins.

When we needed the truth most, it remained far from us.

Instead, we heard the same thing over and over: "The girls are fine."

Years later, when I asked why no one had shared the plain truth of hope in Jesus with us during that time, a friend told us that perhaps our community already saw us as good people. Perhaps they thought we didn't need the message of Christ's salvation for *us*. But they couldn't have been more wrong.

We'd grown up Amish and lived our whole lives for God … the only problem was we did not know Him. Not in a way we later discovered we could.

CHAPTER 3

Growing Up Amish

IRENE

I couldn't imagine being anything other than Amish. It's all we knew, and it's all our parents, grandparents, and great-grandparents before us knew. On both sides of our family we descended from the Amish. Well, mostly. Ora Jay has a unique family member. A distant grandfather was actually born *Englisch* but was adopted into an Amish family as a boy. Great-grandpa lost his non-Amish dad when he was six years old, and an Amish man stopped by on his way home from town and took him home to live with his family. He was raised Amish and became a member later.

Our family's Descendants Book contains a lot of information, and it's amazing to know the histories of our families. My mother's side came to the United States from Germany and Switzerland in the 1770s. In 1785 one of my descendants went west to Indiana on horseback. He sold his horse for a down payment on some property and then walked back to get the rest of the family. Most of our ancestors — from both sides — moved to Pennsylvania from Europe.

I also have an Amish relative that many Amish know about . . . and no doubt many Amish are related to! Here is how my relative Jacob Hochstetler's story is shared in the book *Amish Grace*:

> The Amish are a story-telling people, and perhaps the best-known story in Amish circles is that of Jacob Hochstetler, an eighteenth-century Amish man who lived with his family on the Pennsylvania frontier. In 1757, as the French and Indian War reached their corner of the world, the Hochstetlers awoke one night to find Native Americans attacking their cabin. Two of Hochstetler's sons, Christian and Joseph, reached for their hunting guns, but Jacob would have none of it; he forbade them to use violence. Instead, the family took refuge in the cellar. The mother, one son, and one daughter were killed. Two of the surviving sons later fathered large families, from which a sizable percentage of today's Amish population can trace its ancestry — no doubt one of the reasons the story is so often repeated.*

Indeed, I grew up hearing that story as well as many other stories about Amish martyrs. As small children we were taught how our ways of nonviolence and humility were the right ways. I had no reason to doubt that the Amish way was the one right way to live.

For all of our growing-up years, Ora Jay and I lived in LaGrange County, near the town of LaGrange, Indiana. It is the second largest Amish community in the country, but to us it was always just home.

The first Amish settlers moved into the Shipshewana – LaGrange County area in 1844, having moved from Pennsylvania, and their presence seeped into every part of the community. If you head in any direction you will find yourself driving along country roads dotted with Amish homes. You'll see simple homes, mostly white or gray,

---

*Donald B. Kraybill, Steven M. Nolt, and David L. Weaver-Zercher, *Amish Grace*: *How Forgiveness Transcended Tragedy* (San Francisco: Jossey-Bass, 2007), Kindle Edition, 1587 – 88.

expansive fields, barns, clotheslines, and large gardens. You can't go a mile without coming upon an Amish buggy on the road. Some are open wagons and others are buggies with tops. You may spot children in a cart pulled by a pony. In town Amish women work in the restaurants and gift shops. Within these shops you'll find hand-crafted Amish furniture, quilts, toys, and other handmade items, and the area has become a tourist destination.

You get a sense of peace as you drive along the country roads of LaGrange County. The slow pace of a buggy gives you time to think, to take in the views, and to wave to neighbors and friends riding by in buggies heading the opposite direction.

I grew up knowing all our neighbors. Each Amish community is broken into districts, with about 120 people to a district. We attended church with those who lived closest to us. These were the people we shared our lives with. Although the Amish are considered a private people to *Englischers*, there is nothing private about living within an Amish community. Everyone knows about everyone else — how could you not when you gather together for church every other week, work alongside each other, and even spend time together at quilting circles and barn raisings, which we call "frolics."

Both Ora Jay and I were from what are considered smaller families in the Amish community. Ora Jay, born in 1955, is the second of five children. Esther Ferne, David Lee, Ida Mae, and Daniel Ray are his siblings.

Ora Jay's father was the youngest of twelve children. By the time Ora Jay was old enough to remember his grandparents, they were both gentle white-haired people who offered him candy as he cuddled on their laps. They lived seven miles away, down a long lane. Their house had a big bank barn, a silo, and a children's playhouse.

A water system was run with the help of a windmill. It not only ran water to the house, but it also cooled the milk cans.

As in all Amish families, Ora Jay's grandparents lived in the back of the main house in a *dawdy* house. Uncle Noah and his family lived in the main house, and with the help of the family, Grandpa and Grandma would be cared for all their days. That's the way it works with the Amish. You're born into the Amish, and you die the same. The community takes care of each other. Families stay united. Growing up, I knew only a few people who had left, but I never understood why anyone would want to.

Ora Jay remembers a time when his family traveled during a snowstorm. The drifts in the road were so bad that the buggy got stuck. The lunging horse broke the shafts trying to pull it out, so they had to walk the rest of the way home. Many family memories are centered on the family buggy.

Ora Jay's father tried farming for a time, but it didn't work out so he went to work in a local trailer factory. Many people believe the Amish farm is able to care for all their needs. That wasn't the case fifty years ago, and it's not the case today. In fact, farming is even harder now. With land being divided up, most Amish men run a small farm and work outside the home. People believe that the Amish lifestyle has stayed the same for hundreds of years, and while that is true in some cases, things change. Things always change.

Many people don't realize the differences between Amish communities. Some are more conservative, others more liberal. For example, bicycles weren't allowed in the district where Ora Jay lived as a boy, yet they were allowed in the district where Ora Jay's Uncle Neal lived. Going to visit his uncle was like visiting a different world; the boys would jump onto those bikes and ride for hours. His parents didn't say anything as long as no one else was around.

Back home, the boys knew better than to ask for a bicycle. It just wasn't allowed, and Ora Jay never questioned it. He didn't think to ask why bicycles were allowed at his uncle's place and not his. Amish kids are raised to be obedient and not to ask questions. If they did ask a question they'd get a simple answer, "Someday you'll understand." That's how things are. You do what you do because that's how things are done. Sometimes when you get older you still don't understand why, but it doesn't matter. Obedience to the bishop, parents, and community is just as important when one is older as obedience to one's parents is when one is young.

My growing-up years were similar to Ora Jay's in some ways but different in others. I was one of six girls, and our parents were older when they got married. My parents had the same birthday and were married on the day they both turned twenty-seven. I was the second oldest, and my sisters are Mary Anna, Wilma, Ida Mae, Luella, and Katie.

I remember when my younger sisters were born, especially Katie. I wanted to name her Katie Marie, but *Mem* just named her Katie, with *Dat's* middle initial E.

Dat had an engine shop, and he worked on gas engines used on the farm. Occasionally he would fix lawnmowers for the *Englisch* too. We could only use push mowers in our community, but *Dat* would often run the gas mowers over a few swaths of our lawn, just to test them.

Dat was a man of few words and loyal to all the rules. He never joked around like my grandfather. Grandpa was always saying funny things, and I loved going to his and Grandma's house, which was three miles away.

In addition to working full-time, *Dat* became a preacher when I was young. Most people don't know that a preacher is chosen by lot.

First, members of the local congregation are nominated; then the men who are nominated leave the room. A pile of songbooks is set out — one for each man — and a Scripture verse is placed into one of the books. The men return one at a time and choose a book. The man with the book with the inserted Scripture is chosen to be the preacher.

The Amish believe God chooses the preacher in this way. Even so, life changes for that man and his family. In addition to having to preach, more is expected from him. His life and his family are set up as role models, and for some, that is hard. The work involved has to be done in addition to their ordinary jobs and family life. Like the apostle Paul, they do not stop working at their other jobs to become ministers. Instead, ministering becomes an extension of their jobs and lives.

Amish preachers wear no special garb or insignia. They tend their fields and barns and make their livings as farmers and factory workers. On Sunday, however, these men stand before others just like them. When an Amish minister shares from God's Word, he backs it up with day-to-day concerns from his own life. His preaching isn't one of concepts, but of experience, and the messages are often those that have been passed down through tradition rather than studied in God's Word. For many preachers, Bible study is something to add on to an already busy week, and reading the Bible in German isn't easy if one never learned the language.

Ora Jay and I grew up with one friend who became a preacher when he was still quite young. He was expected to preach in German, but he had little knowledge of the Bible and had a hard time reading German. He had a steep learning curve to prepare himself, but at least he had other preachers to lean on for support and help. Every congregation has four preachers, and they take turns preaching. The sermons are quite lengthy.

In the same way as a preacher is chosen, a bishop is chosen by lot as well. Our friend became the bishop, and this was even harder. The bishop in each district considers the opinion of the other preachers, and the bishop has the final say concerning all issues that arise. People go to him for all the decisions on how to do things — what's allowed and what's not allowed.

"If you have to question if it's right or not — just don't do it," is a common saying of many bishops. They marry and bury people and are always the ones who baptize. Bishops are expected to speak first at meetings, and they always lead the community in prayer before meals. They are challenged over and over again by those in the community who ask, "Why can't we do things this way?" Mostly, they are supposed to know God's Word better than anyone else, even though they receive no special training for this task.

Can you imagine preaching to a crowd of people when you can't even read the language you are supposed to be preaching in? Wouldn't you be concerned if you couldn't even live up to what you needed to be as a preacher or a bishop? Of course, this wasn't something we thought of during our early years. Things just were as they were.

Amish church services are always the same. They are held in a barn, shed, or house. Growing up, I remember the smell of hay on my Sunday clothes and watching the other girls come in, excited that they'd soon be sitting by me.

The preachers would come in first, before any of the other men, and shake hands with all the women. A few would shake hands with the children sitting with their *mems*. That would take longer, but the men who did that were considered more righteous. Of course, even when they shook hands with everyone it was more like just getting the job done. The preachers often didn't even look into the faces or say a word ... but everyone would know if he missed a person.

When you went to church, quite a fuss was made not to be the last family to arrive, and if you were late, you always let everybody know the reason — you had a fresh cow or the horses had gotten out of a broken fence or the sow had piglets.

A lot of Amish morals and values came from the Pathway Press magazines, such as *Family Life*, published in Aylmer, Ontario. Stories were printed about chewing gum in church or a family's conversations in the morning before church about daily work (talking about such things on church day was carnal). Magazines like this reminded us that spiritual talk was sharing concerns about a sick person or an accident or helping young people to be better. Phrases like "Flying *kapp* strings on the way to hell" insinuated that one's *kapp* strings should be tied and not just hanging loose.

Growing up Amish, I was always well provided for. I felt loved, even though I don't remember my parents telling me that. There was a security about the way we lived. All that security came from church rules. If you followed the rules, you got the impression you were doing okay and would go to heaven.

We always had our meals — breakfast, dinner, and supper — precisely at the same time each day. School was a one-room Amish schoolhouse. A neighbor girl would pick us up in her pony and cart, and we'd go about a mile.

When many people think of the Amish, they think about children walking barefoot or riding their ponies to an Amish school. In earlier years, both Ora Jay and I went to school on a school bus. We attended a public school taught by *Englisch* teachers, but all the kids were Amish. That was the only thing available in our community.

It's all we knew. At school we played a lot of ball and Ping-Pong. Our schoolrooms were heated by a woodstove, and we went to the bathroom in outhouses.

In 1961 I entered first grade at a one-room public schoolhouse, Sand Hill School, where grades one through four were taught. Mrs. Seigly was my first- and second-grade teacher, and Mrs. Thelma Keenan was my third- and fourth-grade teacher. In 1965, when I passed to fifth grade and attended Taylor School, Mrs. Margarite Colby was my teacher for the upper grades five through eight. Like Sand Hill School, Taylor School had all Amish students but an *Englisch* teacher — one teacher for four grades.

I didn't attend Taylor all four years. In August 1967 the public schoolhouses were closed, so the Amish got permission from the state to put up their own one-room schools, called Amish parochial schools. The one in our area was Meadow Lane, where I started attending seventh grade. One special boy was in the sixth grade that year. His name was Ora Jay Eash.

Mary Arlene Byler was our teacher, and I continued going to school there my eighth- and ninth-grade years. In all Amish communities, students stop going to school in the ninth grade, at age fourteen. Ninth grade in our school consisted of vocational classes, so we did our work at home and then brought our homework to school only on Fridays.

Amish students do not go to high school. The Amish believe that by age fourteen you need to start learning adult responsibilities. Young women stay home and help their mothers or work as *maudes* and help women in their community. Young men learn a trade or get a job.

Yet even when a person gets a job, he or she doesn't keep any of the money. Most of the income goes to the parents to help support the family, and the young worker gets an allowance, maybe a couple of dollars. This continues until the child is "of age," which is twenty or twenty-one years old. In our community a lot of young people went to work in trailer factories. In the ninth grade Ora Jay worked for a second cousin on his farm.

In 1970, I was sixteen years old, the *rumspringa* age for Amish youth. I was now old enough to start going with the young fellows, but I'd already decided I wasn't going to be one of those "wild" girls. Of course, I did make my Amish dresses a little fancier and nicer, but I never did "rat" my hair, which was the fad among the more popular girls in that era.

It is common for Amish boys in *rumspringa* not to dress Amish at all. Girls usually do, unless they go to parties and such. If Amish girls are seen around town in *Englisch* clothes, the word gets out, "There wasn't a thread of Amish on her."

On Sunday nights I gathered with other men and women from the community at the youth sing. There were more than twenty young men, but I was only interested in one. We gathered around the tables where we sat to eat, boys on one side and girls on the other. After we finished, the plates were cleared, and then we would sit down with our hymnbooks to sing. The hymns were mostly in English, although it was more righteous to sing the German songs that we sang at church. They were the same songs that our parents and grandparents had sung as youths, as well as many generations of Amish before them. Of course we'd sing them at a faster tempo. Our music was nothing like the kind you heard in grocery stores, played with musical instruments. That just wasn't allowed.

I didn't think much about the words slipping from my lips. Instead, I thought of Ora Jay. Was he thinking of me? I glanced up, and our eyes met across the table. Heat rose to my cheeks, and I quickly looked away. I focused my attention on the hymnbook in my hands. I reached up to make sure every hair was tucked away under my *kapp*. Other young men and women were more obvious with their flirtations, but I wasn't about to draw attention to myself in such a way. Snacks were brought out, and we lined up to get them just as the sun made its last descent over the horizon.

In March 1971, Ora Jay and I started dating. We spent a lot of time at his house or mine on weekends, and then we would go to the Sunday sings. Ora Jay was handsome, and he would watch for his chance to take me home from a sing. Sometimes on a Sunday evening he and his buddy would come to my house to visit. Later he told me he went all that way just to get a glimpse of me. I was excited when he asked me for a real date. One weekend we went to a concert at Buck Lake Ranch in Angola, Indiana, where Dolly Parton and Porter Wagoner were performing. That was something special!

I enjoyed spending time with Ora Jay, but he had a bit of a wild streak. He had a new horse, a new buggy, and new clothes, and he even had an eight-track player in his buggy. Together we would go out and gather with other young people at a store called Emmatown. We'd tie up our horses and hang out. The wilder youths in the community would go to the LaGrange Theater. Watching movies, of course, was something that was preached against. The preachers made it sound as if it was the awfullest place in the world. Later, Ora Jay would joke, "I couldn't have dragged Irene in there if I had to."

In October 1971, just a few months after I started dating Ora Jay, my *dat* was ordained bishop. He had been ordained minister eleven years earlier to the day, when I was only six years old. The only thing I remember about his being ordained minister was that my *mem* had just had a baby so she hadn't gone to church. Now, since I was in the *rumspringa* age, I didn't attend church when my *dat* became bishop. (It's not frowned upon so much unless you are a member of the church.) It was an all-day service, and in the evening a lot of people came to our house. It was a solemn and serious time, almost like a funeral.

A bishop is the ultimate example. They stand out in dress, demeanor, and stature. They can't play sports with the other men or even have a light conversation. Bishops are sober and serious, and they encourage others to live the good lives they are called to.

Living a good life — a godly life — was more important than anything in our home. And being Amish, we felt that only we knew the true way. We had kept ourselves from the world, as Scripture says we should. And as long as we stayed on the straight and narrow path, we had hope that our deeds would claim us a place in heaven.

CHAPTER 4

Saying Good-bye

IRENE

Ora Jay and I started a "steady" relationship. That meant we were now committed to each other — seeing each other every weekend, plus a few times in between. If one of us was invited to a wedding, social gathering, or other event, the other one would be automatically invited too. In this type of relationship, breaking up is still an option, but it's not an option after marriage. There is no divorce in an Amish community.

Many Amish young people turn earnestly to the question of family and marriage in the year after receiving the sacrament of baptism. Or another way to think of it is that when Amish young people are interested in marriage and family, they know that baptism is a first step.

Baptism into the church is one of the foundations of Amish faith. It was their desire to fulfill the believer's baptism as adults that first distinguished our ancestors from other believers. As they pulled away from the state church, Anabaptists were imprisoned and exiled, fined, and threatened. This is when they first separated themselves, and the separation continues today.

Baptism — the sign of church membership and commitment — is only for adults or those old enough to choose the path of discipleship. When a young man or woman decides to join the church, he or she usually does so with a group of other young people. Once the bishop is informed, instruction classes begin. The classes teach the foundations and Scriptures of the Amish faith. Lessons begin late spring or in the fall and continue through the summer or winter.

Baptism is an outward sign of an inward conviction to believe in the Lord Jesus Christ and to join the church. In the Amish church, seasons come and seasons go, but with the coming of late spring, mothers and fathers pray that their young adult children will choose *this* season to be baptized.

When a young Amish person chooses baptism, he is choosing to give up his own life for God's life, and his own will for God's will by putting oneself under the Amish Rules.

Ora Jay and I were both baptized when we were eighteen. I grew up knowing I wanted to be a member. I had already joined the church first, but since I was always submissive to the rules, I knew I needed to take the step of baptism as well. I never wanted to do anything out of order.

I remember that day well. After the hymns and sermons, I knew it was time. At the preacher's direction I approached the front and kneeled on a rag carpet that the woman of the house had put there.

"You are making a promise to God, as witnessed by the church. If you still feel the same, you can repeat after me: '*Ja*, I believe Jesus Christ is the Son of God.'" These were the words I was told to say. These are the words I *wanted* to say.

Next came the three questions that everyone is asked when they are baptized.

"Do you believe and trust that you are uniting with a Christian church of the Lord, and do you promise obedience to God and the church?" the preacher asked.

"*Ja.*"

"Do you renounce the devil, the world, and the lustfulness of your flesh and commit yourself to Christ and His church?"

"*Ja.*"

"Do you promise to live by the standards, the *Ordnung,* of the church, and to help administer them according to Christ's Word and teaching, and to abide by the truth you have accepted, thereby to live and thereby to die with the help of the Lord?"

"*Ja.*"

The preacher then removed the prayer covering from my head. I lifted my chin, and one of the other preachers approached, holding a pitcher filled with fresh, clear water. One preacher poured water into the other preacher's hands. I closed my eyes. Warm water was poured down over my head three times. The baptism was done just as it had been done for my *mem* and *dat.* Just as it had been for my grandparents and great-grandparents. Just as it had been for generations of Amish.

"In the name of the Father, the Son, and the Holy Ghost," the preacher said. The preacher cleared his throat. "In the name of the Lord and the church, we extend to you the hand of fellowship. Rise up, and be a faithful member of the church."

I quickly wiped the water off my face and then rose. The preacher's wife approached and placed a holy kiss on my lips as a sign that I was one of them. I stopped wearing my fancy dresses and went back to the simple Amish clothes. I was thankful to now be a part of them.

Ora Jay followed suit about six months later, out of submission. When a young man gets baptized, he gets a new suit coat (called *mutza*) made with a slot in the back, a sign that you are a member.

Things were happening just as I'd always planned and expected, and once I was baptized I began looking at the future ahead.

On September 19, 1974, when I was twenty years old, Ora Jay and I got married in a neighbor's shop. It's normal to have the "wedding church" in an outside building if the weather is warm enough. This gives folks more room, and it's not as stuffy as in a house. (The Amish do not have air conditioning, after all.) The wedding church ceremony is basically the same as a regular church service and lasts for three hours.

A reception followed the wedding church and was held at my home place. Almost all the furniture was removed from the house the week before, and tables were set up for the wedding dinner, which is a full-course meal. Most of the guests are invited for the evening meal too, which we called supper. It too is a full-course meal with a different menu.

In the Amish community there is no such thing as a honeymoon; the next day we got to wash dishes from the evening before! The custom is that the *nâvâ huckers* (which means "side sitters") help with the dishes and getting things back in order. We chose two couples as *nâvâ huckers*, whose role is similar to that of bridesmaids and groomsmen. They sat on either side of us during the meals and also during the wedding ceremony.

We also chose couples to be our "table waiters." Some we stuck together as couples. Others were friends who already had "steadys." They served the tables when we ate, and they sat at the bridal table in the evening.

We didn't go away together after our wedding. Instead, we moved into the basement of Ora Jay's sister and brother-in-law's rental house.

By May 1975, we were ready for a change. We had a baby on the way, and we were looking to move to a farm for the benefit of our future family. We moved to one in Woodruff, a little ways off the main Amish settlement. We couldn't get a loan, so that fell through. We also discovered that it was just too far away if we wanted to go somewhere in our horse and buggy. We only lived there five months.

August 9, 1975, our first baby was born, and we named her Suetta. Ora Jay had a close neighbor by that name, and he'd spent a lot of time with her brother. I also knew that neighbor quite well and thought a lot of her.

In October we bought forty acres from an *Englisch* man. It was adjacent to Ora Jay's grandpa's land, and we moved into a rental house about a mile from the property. We were excited to start building, but it was a lot of work starting from scratch. We worked on it, and in July of 1976 we moved into the basement of the new house. On February 25, 1977, our second daughter was born. We named her Sarah Mae after my mom.

A boy soon joined our family. On August 30, 1978, Marion was born. He was our third child and first son. He was also the first male on my side, since I had all sisters. He was also the first boy grandchild on both sides.

God had given us much, but we had losses too. In November 1978 my *mem* died of cancer.

On May 22, 1980, Eli Ray was born, our fourth child. We named him after Ora Jay's dad. And sometime in the fall of that year we moved onto the main floor of the house. It felt so spacious after living in the basement with our growing family.

On August 23, 1982, our oldest daughter, Suetta, started school. She went to an Amish one-room school, named Countryside School, about a mile and a half down the road. Now we were school parents. We added this to the list of tasks that we managed, in addition to our work at home, on the farm, and in our church and community. Amish life is a calling in itself. "If you want to be an Amish man, dress right and be prepared to really work" was a common saying. If I heard this once, I heard it a hundred times.

And work is what Ora Jay and I set out to do after we were married. We focused on our house, our things, our family. We worked hard, as good Amish people do. Our lives were busy, and we considered ourselves as living as we should ... until our buggy split into a thousand pieces.

Before that night, we had no idea that life could change so quickly. On August 27, 1982, we lost our girls. We were heartbroken.

ORA JAY

On the day of Suetta and Sarah Mae's funeral, the tears never stopped flowing. Our tears and the tears of those in attendance dropped from cheeks and chins, no matter how much we tried to wipe them away. No one tries to put on a brave face at an Amish funeral. It's a time for mourning, no doubt about that.

The funeral was held in a big shed at the bishop's house, and I suppose nearly a thousand people were there. Most we knew, many we didn't.

Helping out at the funeral were young women who took the coats of the guests and put them on a table. Since all the Amish dress the same, our names were on a label inside the garments, and shawls and bonnets were set aside too. Outside, men were helping with the horses and buggies. They used chalk to number the horses and buggies so they could be matched when it came time to hitch them up. You would often see a buggy with a number on its side, and the driver would tell everyone he'd been at a funeral for someone in the community. A rock grew in my stomach realizing that those numbers represented our daughters. I also thought about how many times I had helped with the horses and buggies. Now I was the grieving family member, something I had never expected.

Still, they came to pay respect. People that we'd never talked to before were shaking our hands and offering their regards. Amish bond together through the seasons of life. A dark day like this was no different.

A funeral is similar to a church service with a sermon and a time to sing hymns. Also, like a church service, the men and women sit separately, sectioned off by age. Only the immediate relatives sit together as a family. After everyone was seated on the long wooden benches with no backs, our family filed in together. It felt good to have my wife and children beside me during this time. Different but good. All around us were muffled cries, the wiping of tears, and blowing noses. My hands trembled on my lap. I wanted to reach out to comfort my wife, but not here. Not now. It wasn't our way.

At a funeral the preacher holds nothing back during his sermon and speaks with reality and fear. The Amish believe that during the age of innocence children go to heaven, but for those older — the future is in God's hands. No one would be prideful enough to claim a spot in heaven for themselves or their family members.

During Amish funerals for adults, the preacher says such things as, "They're one step ahead of us" or "They're probably in heaven." Family members cling to the hope that it is so.

The preacher who spoke at our girls' funeral had recently lost a daughter in an accident, and even though it was not common, he talked about our girls and used their names as he preached. This brought us comfort, and we appreciated his kindness. Moments like that were pinpricks of light through a darkly veiled time and even then brought a bit of healing.

After the preacher had spoken for two hours, we approached the open caskets. It was a time for all those in attendance to file past and pay their last respects.

Unless the accident was extremely bad, there is always a viewing of the deceased before the journey to the cemetery. Each person files past, even the children. Parents lift the little ones up to get a better view. Sometimes the parents have the young ones touch the person's face. Children need to understand the reality of life and death as a reminder to each of us that we must strive to live right, for who knows when our time will come.

After the viewing, we emerged from the shed, and everyone still lingered. A buggy was brought around to us — as is always the case for the family of the deceased — and then the others followed us to the graveyard where one deep hole awaited the small, simple wooden caskets. Suetta's and Sarah Mae's caskets were put into the same hole, buried together just as they had died — side by side, next to Irene's mother.

At the graveside, the preacher shared more words and Scriptures in German, and then he read out of a smaller songbook. As we stood there, huddled as a fragmented family, men from the congregation covered the caskets shovelful by shovelful with earth. The memory of the sound of the clumps of dirt hitting the wooden caskets will never leave my mind.

One special memory is when Irene and I were talking to little Marion and Eli about their sisters' deaths. We told them that Suetta and Sarah Mae were in heaven now. Marion's face brightened, and he said, "Yeah, Sarah Mae said the other day that when she dies she was going to fly to heaven." This gave me peace that God had been preparing the girls.

Since the Amish do not take photographs, two locks of hair — one light, one dark — is all that we have from our daughters. That and the memory of their faces and their smiles. Sometimes we catch an expression or a gesture from one of the other children or grandchildren that reminds us of the girls, but memories fade. Nothing remains the same on this earth, not even what you carry inside.

At the time, our hearts were set more firmly on living right. We had an even greater desire for heaven, for a part of our hearts was already there. It took years for Irene and me to discover that living good was not how we could be confident of our place in heaven. But much happened before then. Many things.

God granted us the ability to feel the ache and hollowness in our souls for a while. But on our journey to find respite, we never expected what came to us. We found Jesus waiting ... as we were never taught He could be.

A promise for our present.

A simple hope for our eternity.

CHAPTER 5

Life without Our Girls

ORA JAY

There is no such thing as "quiet" in the weeks that follow the death of an Amish person. Others in the community owe the family a visit. This isn't planned among the community; it just happens. As I went through the motions of doing chores around our farm, and as Irene went through the motions within the house, we would see a buggy come down the lane, and then another. Four, five, six families would come. In the first month after their death, at any time in the evening, people would just show up.

These were people we shared our lives with, sat next to in church, built barns together with. Our children attended the same school. As each family arrived, the father would tie up the horse to the hitching rack, and the family members would climb off the buggy and just come into the house. No one would knock.

Seeing the buggies come down the lane reminded me of the days before we lost the girls. My parents lived close by, and they would often come over to help as we built the farm. They would come during the evening to help out where they could. As soon as our girls heard the clip-clop of the buggy on the road, with barely a pause they would race barefoot out the front door, letting the screen door slam behind them.

"*Dawdy's* here! *Dawdy's* here! *Dawdy, Dawdy, Dawdy!*"

But now as I heard the clomp of horses' hooves and the squeak of buggy wheels as visitors came, there were no girls' excited cries, no pitter-patter of feet, and the screen door didn't slam. Our visitors entered with solemn looks. We would walk around the farm and chat about everyday things. We knew the loss of Suetta and Sarah Mae was the reason they'd come, yet people rarely mentioned the girls' names. It was very special to us when someone did mention their names.

It was nice having friends stop by, but when they left, the house felt empty. We had friends, but we didn't have the girls. The ones who talked the most about our girls were our siblings, who would share special memories. That meant a lot to us.

The people in our community rallied around us. I'd been doing work on the barn at the times of the girls' deaths, and the men hosted a couple of frolics and finished up the barn. The women also pitched in and helped with the housework and meals. That's the way the Amish show they care, by rolling up their sleeves.

Irene and I continued to go through the motions, but there was a time when I wondered what the point was.

IRENE

In addition to friends stopping by, our mailbox overflowed with hundreds of sympathy cards. Many of them contained poems inside the simple card. Others would write out a Scripture verse. The cards that we read more than once were those that had a personal note inside. Even if we didn't know the person, we searched for hope in their words, almost as if we were looking for answers in those few lines of text.

One of the unexpected gifts was a memorial poem written by an Amish woman we did not know. It meant a lot that people throughout the Amish community were praying for us and remembering our girls. She wrote a stanza of a poem for each letter of their names.

Suetta O. Eash
Born August 9, 1975
Died August 27, 1982
Age 7 years 18 days

Sarah Mae Eash
Born February 25, 1977
Died August 27, 1982
Age 5 years 6 months 2 days

Such a pleasant August evening.
The world lay fast asleep;
Just a typical Friday evening,
A night so calm and deep.
A buggy approached the highway;
Nothing seemed amiss
The horse was trotting homeward;
Good time he made in this.

Unknown to the sleeping girls,
In the corner of the backseat
The death angels were hovering,
There would be no retreat.
How must have been the picture,
Of innocence that night,
When softly stole the death angel,
And gave them not a fright.

Ear did not hear them coming,
For the crash was far too loud.
Then all was brought to a stand-still,
As gathered an anxious crowd.
'Twas then in His Mercy and Kindness,
God claimed two immortal souls
He had designed them only recently,
Now reached their heavenly goals.

To a family these souls were given,
Some recent years before
To be loved, instructed, and wanted,
And cherished and loved some more.
The family was then completed,
When the babies entered the home;
They dreamed of having these babies,
Until they matured and were grown.

Two willing little helpers,
They turned out to be.
Why, they could do the dishes,
And do them cheerfully.
Then one hung out the wash,
While the other mowed the lawn
Then when the chores were done,
They'd play till day was gone.

And then with two little brothers,
What helpers that they were,
Entertaining them for Mom;
Telling stories, too, I'm sure.
But Mom got her turn,
When braiding time was due,
With Bible storybook in hand,
They came for one or two.

And

Such were the happy times,
When pony rides were had,
Flying through the air,
Clinging on to Dad.
The outdoors was great;
What fun to be alive,
No worries, and no cares;
Blessing those who touched their lives.

And then came the day,
Oh great it was and fun,
For seven-year-old Suetta,
When school had just begun.
What a flashing bright smile,
And eyes sparkling blue —
Blond hair freshly combed,
And lunch pail brand-new!

Ready to tell the stories,
In her eager, friendly way;
When she came home from school;
At the end of every day.
The week was short and sweet,
And she had only one,
So soon schoolwork and lessons;
Were completed and were done.

Ah, yes, these little girls,
Enjoyed their cousins, too,
With two on either side,
There were always things to do.
Babies were so delightful,
And fun to love and hold.

Perhaps they have found some;
To cuddle in heaven above.

Hardly seven weeks later,
A little brother came,
To bless the bereaved family,
Danny is his name.
Oh, what would the girls say,
Of such a lovely child?
Wouldn't they just "ah" and "oh,"
And make him coo and smile?

Many are the fond memories,
We cannot all recall.
Although they bring us tears,
We thank God for them all.
We know there's no mistake,
God planned it all just so;
They were too sweet to stay;
And their joys now overflow.

Ah, yes, what more could we wish them,
Free from trials of life,
Free from this world of sorrow;
Free from sin and strife.
They cannot come to us,
But we may go to them;
If we but live for Christ;
We'll surely meet them again.

Each day is a new beginning,
A challenge bright and clean,
But a hole still does remain;
For two we held so dear.
We hear no more their voices.
We see no more their smile;

We've put away their shoes;
We'll meet them after awhile.

Everybody held their breath, when the death message came
Of two girls just five and seven; Suetta and Sarah Mae by name.
"Oh lucky are the girls, in their innocence could go."
But what they couldn't feel, was the cruel, parenting blow.

And then we went to view them, two caskets side by side.
One was blond, the other dark; our tears we could not hide.
Although to man as strangers, the picture was so sweet,
It touched the hearts of hundreds, a story so complete.

So peacefully resting, no hate was ever sown,
No grudges, no ill feelings, no clouds of guilt had known.
Old age had never reached them, no toil on their brow.
No cares marked their foreheads; just tenderness; somehow.

Heaven seemed so much nearer, as we gazed on sleeping ones.
God's call came softly, firmly, our life, too may soon be done.
He chose two lambs to lead us, and show us the way.
If we but follow their footsteps, we'll see the Light of Day!

CHAPTER 6

Seeking a Better Place

IRENE

On October 17, 1982, our fifth child, Danny, was born. As our third son and third living child, Danny was a joy in the midst of our grief and sorrow. Other new family members joined us. On May 23, 1983, my dad got remarried, to a woman named Polly Bontrager who had never been married. On September 11, 1984, LeRoy, our fourth son, was born at home with the help of a midwife. He was a large baby, but all went well.

August 13, 1986, Lester, our fifth son, was born. I had him by C-section since he was 11 pounds, 6 ounces. During this time you would have considered us a typical Amish family. Although we still grieved, the farm, Ora Jay's work at the factory, our children's school, and our church and community life kept us busy — too busy, in a way.

We also received letters from out of state, one of which invited us to be part of an Amish circle letter for those who lost a child. Those letters brought the most healing. Parents would talk about the child they lost. Every time those letters came, Ora Jay and I would sit down and read them. We were always touched by the sentiments and the transparency of the writers. Some families had lost more than one child, and one couple had lost all four of their children in a house fire. Since Ora Jay and I didn't feel we had anyone in our community or family to talk openly to, writing the letters — and reading letters from others — brought a sense of healing.

Ora Jay and I have accumulated many Amish circle letters. We were part of many circles, including the family circle and a circle made up of those who have lost children. The letters would cycle from family to friends, and when a new cycle would begin, we would take out our old letter and replace it with a new one. Sometimes we would copy personal letters before we sent them to family, especially the in-depth letters that we sent later, trying to explain our faith. Those too are included in the book. After the passing of Ora Jay's parents, we were also able to acquire some of the personal letters that we wrote to them. The gathering I am talking about in this letter is a reunion of parents who've lost children in tragic accidents. We were family No. 7 in the group. All letters have been lightly edited.

Circle Letter, Grieving Parents Group

No. 7
Ora Jay Eash Family
September 1, 1986

Dear circling friends,
Greetings in Jesus' holy name.

I want to renew my sheet to this welcome letter which I received last week. I thought I should write as soon as I can so that map from

No. 3's could make some stops yet. Yes, I'm sorry we can't make it again this year. Sure spites me. On August 13 we were blessed with another baby boy named Lester. He weighed eleven pounds and six and a half ounces. I had to have him taken by C-section since he was so big. So takes longer to recover, although I feel pretty good by now. Of course, I tire real easy yet.

My maud is peeling pears right now. I was helping till now when baby woke up, so am nursing him. He has a really stuffy nose — at night it seems a lot worse. Otherwise he is doing alright.

Last night we took LeRoy (almost) age two, up to doctor's office to have his head stitched. He fell off the manure spreader while we had visitors yesterday p.m. It was a pretty deep cut and had so much dirt on the inside, which possibly was even manure so we decided it was probably best in the long run to go to the doctor. We were thankful it wasn't worse. . . .

This is the first whole day of school for Marion again. A little later than usual but had a hard time getting the second teacher but got one the last minute, and she wanted to have about a week to get ready yet, which I don't blame her for. This past week brought back sad memories again. Four years have gone by since we saw our girls last. When I think of what good help I'd have now it's almost overwhelming but just want to think of how much better off they are now. Well, we hope to meet all of you sometime but guess it has to wait.

> Just us,
> The Eash Family

We had everything an Amish family could desire. We had our farm, and Ora Jay worked at a local factory for a good wage. We had five boys, but something didn't seem right. Life was busy. Too busy. We longed for a quieter life, and Ora Jay wanted to find a way to connect with our boys. He'd seen the path other youth had taken — going wild during their *rumspringa* years — and we didn't want that for our sons. That's when Ora Jay started talking about Montana.

Ora Jay's uncle lived there, and he often talked about the secluded place he'd found in the mountains, a place of adventure and beauty. It was a place to leave the rat race of the Amish community of Indiana. In August 1987, Ora Jay and I, along with Marion, Eli Ray, and baby Lester, went by train to visit his uncle Ora for two weeks. Danny and LeRoy stayed with Grandpa Eash.

Being on the train was a new experience for us. I was surprised by how friendly everyone was. This was unexpected. Where we came from in Indiana, the *Englisch* weren't so polite. Then again, the Amish usually weren't polite either. There was a wall between us. A feeling of "us" versus "them." The farther away from Indiana we got, the more attention we received. People would look and stare, and I have to admit I didn't mind it. I was proud of our heritage and our lifestyle. Many times people would ask why we dressed in Plain clothes, and Ora Jay would explain that we were Amish.

We also got many compliments on how well the boys behaved. "Oh, they have to learn how to behave and sit still," I'd say with a smile. "An Amish church service is three hours long!"

We couldn't believe how beautiful Montana was. When the train pulled into Flathead Valley, a different world opened to us outside the window. The neat properties and crisscross of rural roads was far behind us. In Montana, pine trees clung to rocky cliff faces, and a river roared through the base of the canyon. The color of the river water was bluish-green, and white foam danced on the surface, reflecting in the morning light.

As we stepped from the train I cocked my head and lifted it to the wide blue sky. In the distance, hills rose and then turned into mountains. Seeing Ora Jay in Montana, I knew that two weeks wasn't going to satisfy him.

Even though the view was breathtaking, my heart felt a slight pinch, realizing how many miles separated me from the family and friends we loved so much. After two weeks of exploration, I was happy to get home and back to my normal routine.

On November 25, 1988, Gerald, our sixth son, was born, also by C-section. In March 1990 we had another loss when I miscarried.

The loss hit me hard, and it renewed the grief over our girls. For a year I'd let the girls' clothes hang in the closet along with mine and Ora Jay's, until I packed them away. But I was soon to discover that loss was going to build upon loss. Family, church, community — we'd lose so much as Ora Jay set his gaze on Montana.

The two-week vacation in Montana only fueled Ora Jay's desire to live there for a longer period of time. We talked about it and decided we would go for one year, partly for the adventure and partly as a way to connect with our boys before the tumult of *rumspringa*.

Ora Jay's oldest sister Esther and her husband, Ervin, were talking about moving there too. Ervin and Ora Jay had always gotten along well. They used to go fishing and coon hunting together, even though it was frowned upon by many in the community. When some of the other husbands would do the same, their wives would comment, "They were out again when they should have been working." A *tsk-tsk* usually followed that statement. An Amish man has plenty of work to keep him busy without doing things for sport.

But Esther and Ervin never committed to moving, so our family alone was moving to Montana — with me preparing to live in a foreign place with no one I knew and a large family to care for.

I dreaded the move. I didn't know what to expect. We had no family there, and people in our LaGrange community talked against us for even considering moving so far away to such a wild place. Still, I told myself, we were only going to be there a year, and I knew I could make it through that. A year would go by quickly, I hoped.

Circle Letter, Grieving Parents Group

July 28, 1989

Dear friends, known and unknown,

Greetings in Jesus' holy name. "This is the day the Lord hath made. Let us be glad and rejoice in it." The air feels really refreshing this morning. Has of course been hot and humid lately which we can hardly expect anything else at this time of the year....

Want to do the washing again today. Won't be so much since I did it on Tuesday, but too much till next week. Then I have to go grocery shopping today and want to have the baby's shot given. Something that can be put off pretty easy if you don't have an appointment. He's eight months old and was supposed to have it at six months.

Last week there was a sad accident again in this area. A little boy, five years old, died a couple of hours after a wagon full of hay went over him. He was standing on the upright and it broke off and fell on the horses. He fell in front of the wheels and it went over his stomach. He was conscious at the time and first said he didn't want to go to the hospital. Had a lot of pain (stomach) and died about midnight in the hospital of internal injuries. It was Joas, son of William and Ruth (Otto) Yutzy.... They just moved on the farm this spring.

This week one day I and the children went to spend the day with his folks....

The Eashes

ORA JAY

I was looking forward to the adventure of Montana — who wouldn't? The Amish community there is small and intimate, and the mountains frame the small community. There is fresh air and wildlife. I wouldn't have to work in a factory. I could work with my uncle and spend time exploring nature with my boys.

Yet more than the desire for adventure, I was worried about my older sons, who would be teenagers in only a few years. Irene and I saw how the youth in LaGrange County were acting. No parents wanted their youth to do this *rumspringa* wild thing, but they just did it anyway.

Rumspringa, in an Amish community, is a time for the youth — when they turn sixteen. Although these young people aren't encouraged to get a car, many of them do. It's a major time for them. And it happens overnight. One day they are fifteen and living under their parents' rules, and the next day they are sixteen and able to make their own choices. On the first weekend after you turn sixteen, you are expected to do something different — wild.

It's a time of life when you start thinking for yourself. You also start looking for a partner to marry. You start interacting with the opposite sex and attend singings. All the youth have fun and go to each other's homes. Then some start doing more than that, and parents often don't step in to stop the wild behavior, believing that one day their teenagers will see their folly, come back, become a church member, and put all those things behind them. At least that's what they hope.

As our boys got closer to the age of *rumspringa*, I started to worry. We had a good relationship with our sons, but I didn't want any disconnection. I couldn't bear the thought of them doing what the other teens were doing while I stood aside, not having some input into their choices.

From watching the Amish families around me, I could never tell who was going to act wild and who wasn't. Irene and I wanted more assurance. We wanted our sons to do what we were doing — living a right and godly life. We wanted to keep our close connection with them.

Determined to do something, I met with some of the men at the church. I suggested some things that we could do with our sons within our church district, like play ball together. I urged them to find ways for us to narrow the generation gap, but my ideas were quickly shot down. People didn't think it was necessary. "The way we do things was good enough for our ancestors," they would say. "Why change things and challenge what we do today?" Phrases like that are something you hear often in an Amish church.

That distance between the young men and the older men in the church services seemed to be almost expected. First, young people at church have a hard time understanding what is preached. They speak Pennsylvania Dutch at home and English in school, but all the preaching is done in High German. When families arrive at our church homes, the mothers and girls go in first. Then the men enter and greet each other with a handshake and sometimes a holy kiss. The young men would always gather in their own spot, usually around the barn. It was only later — just as the church service was starting — that they'd make their way inside.

The older my boys got, the more the distance grew, and it hurt my heart. I didn't believe our sons would go out in the world and stay there, but we also didn't want them to go through the struggle of the wild running around. Surely there had to be a better place to raise a family. For me, the Amish community in Montana, where my uncle lived, might be that place. Almost everyone in our community would want to go, but nobody actually did it. It's a unique place, and we would often hear adventurous things about it in *The Budget*, with stories of bears finding their ways onto porches and elk taking down clotheslines. I was sure that a small, quiet place like that wouldn't have the same bad influences as back east.

Our two-week visit had proved my belief to be true, but would our family benefit from moving there long-term? I hoped so. But how could we do it? We had the farm — it was busy and seasonal — and there was school. After thinking about it, I was certain we could find a young couple to rent the farm and manage it for a year while we were gone. We finally decided that if we went for one year the boys could go to school there, and we could have a season of peace and connection.

I wanted more for my family. I wanted my sons to know my love, and I wanted us to have a good relationship. Maybe losing the girls had something to do with that. Maybe after the accident I began to understand what truly mattered.

Irene submitted to move to the West Kootenai, Montana, for a year, and then after we got there, she looked forward to going back to Indiana. But as soon as I took a deep breath of that fresh mountain air, I knew it would be a hard place to leave.

CHAPTER 7

Montana!

ORA JAY

We made it to Montana in May 1990. The West Kootenai area is exactly what you picture when you think of a rural logging community. Winding mountain roads take you high into the hills. In the northwest corner of the state, you find mountain pastures lined with pine and larch trees. Houses dot the landscape here and there, but the wildness cannot be subdivided and controlled. No one wants that.

A sign at the West Kootenai Kraft and Grocery claims Canada is only two miles away. An easy hike. The Kootenai Indians were the first inhabitants, and the area still boasts mountainous views and the abundant water and wildlife that American Indians enjoyed. Amish in this area like to hunt and fish. In fact, in addition to the locals, who live here year-round, twenty to thirty Amish bachelors move to the area each spring so that they can earn their resident hunting licenses by the fall. They stay in bachelor cabins, and many Amish men back east are jealous of their adventures.

The first white men in the area were fur traders in the early part of the nineteenth century. The train came through around 1901, and in 1967 work started on the Libby Dam, which formed Lake Koocanusa.

The name *Koocanusa* came from three words: *Kootenai*, *Canada*, and *USA*. The water from the newly formed lake flooded towns in the area. Since homes, ranches, and businesses in the area had to be evacuated, settlers in the valley relocated higher into the mountains. This mountain settlement was first discovered by Steve Kauffman, a young Amish man in his early twenties. He'd gone west hoping to find land for an Amish settlement. A real estate agent told him about a 2,700-acre ranch for sale across from Rexford, Montana, in an area referred to as the West Kootenai. In 1975 the ranch was purchased by three Amish men, and they, in turn, planned to sell parcels to other Amish looking for a quieter, more isolated lifestyle. Soon Amish families began arriving and settling there, including my uncle. Unable to farm the area where they now lived, many turned to logging and working in small sawmills. Some men raised cattle and became ranchers. They left behind farms, families, and communities in the East. Now we would be doing the same.

IRENE

I was reluctant to move away from our family. I had never gone far from our home in Indiana. I was a homebody. But since Ora Jay was adventurous, we agreed we wanted to get away from the rat race of his trying to farm and do factory work at the same time, in addition to attending all the social gatherings.

Before I knew it, Ora and I stood with our six boys at the train station. I'd carefully packed twelve boxes — two for each of us. I had to pack wisely because everything I supposed we would need for a year was inside those boxes. I couldn't help but think of the girls, about their headstone in the Amish cemetery. I wondered if we'd be making this trip if they were still alive. Most likely not. They'd be in their *rumspringa* years, spending time with friends and catching the eye of potential suitors.

Life had changed for us yet again. Only this time it was our choice. One year from now, maybe, things would be back to the normal life I'd always dreamed of living.

The boys bounced with excitement as we arrived at the train station. Little Lester held tightly to my hand. We had just left Ora Jay's parents back at their home. His *mem* had cried and his father had been somber. This was the first time any of their children had moved so far away, and it wasn't easy for them. I have to admit it wasn't easy for us either.

We got to the station early, so we had time to walk. We strolled for a while, and when it grew closer to the time to board the train, we returned to discover that someone had taken our food cooler with all the goodies for our meals on the train!

A whistle blew in the distance and bodies moved into motion. Passengers lined up, including us. Our things were tucked away in the cargo hold.

It almost seemed like a dream when the train pulled out of the station. I'd never lived so far from home before, and I wondered what waited on the other end of the train ride.

It's only for a year, Irene, I told myself. *You can do anything for one year.* My hope was that Ora Jay would get this Montana dream out of his system. He'd been aching for something different — for something to give him satisfaction — for a very long time. We had the farm we'd always dreamed of and six boys, but I could see a longing in his gaze for something more. I wondered if he could see it in mine too.

We boarded the train. Gerald sat on my lap. Marion sat next to me, his eyes wide as he took in the people on the train. He leaned up and looked out the window. I had to admit that I had a sense of wonder too. I was used to being with my family — my parents and siblings — and Ora Jay's family and our friends. I fiddled with my *kapp* strings and tried to have a normal conversation with Ora Jay.

The train started with a lurch and butterflies danced in my stomach. My body pressed back into my seat, and I hoped that things wouldn't change too much during the year we were gone.

The trip took two days, while the train stopped at various stations. Thankfully, we had another basket with dry foods like bread, chips, and ketchup, so we ate chip sandwiches during our adventure. The boys didn't seem to mind at all!

At the end of our long journey the train screeched to a halt, and it seemed as if all the weariness of the travel faded as the boys jumped from their seats. Montana!

The train took us into Whitefish, where Ora Jay's uncle waited. He saw the pile of boxes we'd brought with us and scratched his head.

"You won't fit all those in that van," Uncle Ora commented.

"Oh, I think I will," Ora Jay countered, knowing that the van had a rack on top.

It was a two-hour drive to the West Kootenai area, and when we arrived I was greeted by the fresh smell of mountain streams and evergreens. It was dark when we got to the rental house, the dim lamps were lit, and I was happy to discover that Uncle Ora had prepared everything for us. He'd even laid out mattresses on the floor. Settling my head on my pillow, I felt a sense of freedom I hadn't expected. It was a welcome feeling.

Letter to Family

May 19, 1990

Dear folks at home,

Greetings in Jesus' name. How does this find you? We are fine. Irene just started with breakfast so thought maybe I could write and let you know how things are or when to travel, etc. We had to wait two hours at Elkhart because train was late, but in Chicago we didn't wait at all. We got to Whitefish at 1:00 a.m., which was late.

There was a van driver there with a rack on top, so we managed to get it all on top and inside, but had a load. We got here at 4:15. They had a light burning so things went pretty good. This is the house where Andy's [Andy Yoder's family] used to live. The house has lots of room, has a porch all the way around, which makes a place for the boys to play.

The boys just all got up. It's 8:09. Got up late ourselves. We have a cook stove that Mike's had but don't have any stovepipes yet. There's a homemade stove in basement that we use to heat with. We went to Kalispell yesterday. With Uncle Ora's. It's ninety-five miles. We got two complete beds, two kitchen chairs, recliner, and bicycle for $130. Stopped at a greenhouse and got some big tomato plants and seeds and flowers; then we stopped at Kmart and got some things. So we spent plenty yesterday.

They put a table here and two school benches for use, and a rocking chair that goes back too far. Ha! Sewing and washing machine. There's also a peacock here that is John Miller's. They have a sandbox and playhouse. Irene went out to house by the road, which is the shop and house Andy's used to live in first. She found a high chair that is usable. That's where the garden is. We spaded some ground in the greenhouse last night. Breakfast is ready, so have to go. I'll let Irene finish this after breakfast.

Hello,

This is past 9:00 now (10:00 your time) — and boys are not quite done washing dishes. I really would have liked to wash today but have no rinse tubs yet and it's just not ready to wash, and being it's Saturday I couldn't get the wash away by tonight.

It has rained off and on every day but the sun shines in between. Ora went out to put up the mailbox. He just made one out of wood. Since we were gone to Kalispell all day yesterday he didn't get it up then. The boys were all at Uncle Ora's yesterday. Then they said we got the Standard [weekly newspaper from Indiana] already. The mailman just left it there. Uncle Ora's had a chicken-barbeque dinner last night for the youngie [youth in the area], so they wanted to be back by 4:00 p.m.

We have to go get groceries sometime today but don't know for sure how we'll go yet. We got a used wagon yesterday. Now the handle is broke off already. Uncle Ora's buggy was damaged with a runaway horse — nobody hurt. He was tied to hitch rack for a while, then got loose.

It wasn't too bad the night we came. They had mattresses on the floor — enough for us all with sheets on, so we had to dig out our comforters and quilts. Was sure glad they had a light burning, as we just had one small flashlight and wasn't sure where the mantels are and no kerosene for lamps. We had gotten a little groceries at Whitefish, so we had something for breakfast. We got worktable stuff about all organized till late dinner. In the afternoon I did the clothes stuff — assorted in boxes for now.

Gerald has been very brutzich [fussy], guess he feels it's not right. But the other boys seem to have adjusted alright for now. They'll probably mind it later more than Gerald does then.

Wonder how David is getting along? Has he had any problems? Hope not. How is everyone in the family? This morn it sounded like we had a dog upstairs. It was Eli Ray with a bad cough. They all slept upstairs last night since we got the beds yesterday. Well, must get to work. Floor needs mopping but have no mop. Don't know if I want to crawl all over with a rag. Well, so long, write also.

Irene and all-in-all

P.S. *The boys said it really hailed yesterday while we were gone. Nights are very cool yet.*

I forgot to pay Dad for those groceries he got for us on Monday. Just made a guess what it was.

Circle Letter, Grieving Parents Group

August 26, 1990

Dear circling friends,

Greetings to you all in Jesus' name! Wonder how this finds you all in different states? Here we are healthy and have lots to be thankful for. It is different out here than what we were used to in Indiana. Weather-wise you just don't have the humid, sticky weather. Although it gets hot for a couple of weeks in the daytime right in the sun. But cools off nights. But then you can also see why the growing season is not so good. As the tomatoes and sweet corn hardly make it till the first frost. I guess they generally have a long, nice, and warm spell after the first frost, but that one is killing and stops the growing for a lot of things. They can expect one around full moon, which is a week and a half away yet....

Yes, we have been enjoying it out here. After we got adjusted. Think Mom had the hardest time.

We have been having a lot of visitors in the area from all over. In the last couple of months there's hardly a time that there's not some strangers here. This last week there's a young couple here that were our neighbors in Indiana, and we've been spending quite a bit

*of time with them. They invited us over for supper. They're staying
in a cabin. We are expecting both of our parents sometime this fall.
Maybe some of our schivistered [siblings]. My sister that's single was
here a month ago.*

*Do you PA folks know John Allgyer's? They came about two
weeks ago, and he will be the school teacher. They are childless.
School will start tomorrow. John has an unmarried uncle, David
Beiler, living out there. There are thirteen families here.*

So Long,
Ora Jay and Irene Eash,
and boys

*P.S. Tomorrow eight long years ago we parted with our beloved
daughters.*

Circle Letter, Grieving Parents Group

December 27, 1990

Dear circling friends,
Greetings of love from the West Kootenai Valley, Montana.

*Wonder how this would find each of you on this snowy winter
eve? Hardly with as much snow as we have here. Maybe, we can
never tell. It is around 20 degrees today, really snowing at times. The
pine trees were really covered, and all the fence posts had ice cream
cones on top (the way the boys say). Then tonight it was getting
a little windy and snowing some more. Is quite deep. They were
predicting a blizzard and temperature to drop pretty low. Last week
we had some sub-zero weather. 26 degrees below the lowest, but it
was not too bad. Although we could not keep the house cozy but was
a lot better than being on the outside!*

*Congratulations to the families with the new babies. Also hope
the unfortunate are better again or almost recovered. We had not*

heard about Leon, No. 10, till you wrote us. John Allgyer's Lydia Ann said she had known it, though. Yes, John is the teacher at the school here. Seems the pupils all like him. They had their Christmas program on Monday eve. Recited poems and sang songs. Thought they all did well. Only fourteen pupils and they had it ringing in there! John says he thinks they're so energetic and eager. Sure like to see it better that way than if dread going to school. (John and Lydia Ann now bought a place out here so guess they are staying.)

No. 9 sounds like you have some sad memories of '90. We never know what the new year of '91 will bring and is probably good we don't. We got to know Ernie Miller and Delmer Schrock from your area. (They were here all summer.) Ernie said he helped on your house this spring. Delmer's folks, Harvey's, were also here this summer. I had known them before this as they used to live in Indiana. Harvey Jr. goes with one of our former close neighbors in Indiana. She had come along out here.

Yes, we like it out here in some ways but of course has some drawbacks. Our plans are to go back in spring. Now, we did not bring all our things along. We came on train so brought no furniture. Ora Jay works for his uncle Ora Miller on the log home business, which is kinda slack at this time of the year. I saw this Irene Brenneman once in Eureka but didn't talk with her. Too bad she's not Amish anymore.

Sheet's full. Can add another one about us.

Ora Jay, Irene, and all

CHAPTER 8

A New Type of Church

ORA JAY

On our first morning in Montana the boys were eager to explore the woods around our rented home. The older boys were ten and twelve. All six of them loved the outdoors, biking, fishing, and horseback riding. They loved the mountains. When we would go hiking, we couldn't hang on to them — they'd be gone so fast. In Shipshewana we used to go down the road to visit relatives or neighbors, but that was as far as we would walk. Or perhaps we'd play some ball or have a little bit of yard play, but it was nothing like being in the mountains. We had plenty of time for exploring.

In Indiana we had a farm; I also worked outside of the home. We were usually busy building buildings or going to community activities, but there were hardly any moments for play. In Montana our rented house needed very little upkeep, and the evenings were long. So we were outside for six to eight hours a day. We had a lot of time for family. We enjoyed life together.

Not only was the place different, but the people were different too. The Amish in Montana chose to dress in a more conservative way. The men wore vests, which is considered more spiritual, and the women wore capes on the upper part of their dresses. This too was considered more righteous because the cape covered a woman's form. We were impressed by how the Amish in Montana had chosen this more spiritual way. The church services impressed us too.

First, there was something to be said about the environment. Since the community is small and rural, most Amish walk to the house church instead of driving a buggy. We would walk down dirt roads and through the woods to go to church. The air was fresh, and the birdsongs would carry us along.

They had a church service every other week, which is traditional, and they followed the same cycle of Scripture verses that all the Amish use. These tell the preachers what Scriptures to use, at what time of the year, and yet there were no Amish preachers in the church in the West Kootenai.

Our friends and family in Indiana had told us about the lack of preachers before we left for Montana. "Don't go," more than one person had told us, "there isn't a preacher ... it's dangerous."

Yet in Montana, the church service was more similar than different. Each family took a turn hosting the gathering — also like back at home; the only difference was it was expected that whoever would have church in their homes would read the Scriptures and everyone was to expound on it.

This made me nervous. I had never wanted to be a preacher, and I wasn't looking forward to having the task now. How was I going to be able to read the Bible ... and expound on the passages?

I remember the first time church took place in our home. I was expected to read the Scriptures and preach, which made my stomach tense, but I had practiced what I wanted to say. I had grown up in church, so I knew the church talk. Even though I spoke to the congregation in Pennsylvania Dutch, there are words one uses in church that aren't used anywhere else.

I said my piece, and then attention turned to the oldest man in the room. Because there was no preacher, each man — starting with the oldest — had a chance to share. The men always started by agreeing with the words of the previous man, and then they would give their own bit of insight.

This fascinated me. It was the first time Irene and I had heard others talk in church besides the preacher. We learned many new insights as we listened to our brothers share what the passage meant to them.

Of course, not everyone appreciated this. Throughout the year — mostly in the summer — Amish visitors would come from all over the United States. The men were both shocked and bothered by the practice of ordinary men in the congregation being asked to say something. Some of the men who visited were fifty or sixty years old and had never been asked to say something in church. Some didn't stay for the weekend on purpose for fear of having to speak.

I remember when my own *dat* visited. It was the first time he'd ever been asked to say something. He could hardly say anything. How could he when he didn't know the church language and the more spiritual ways of talking?

There wasn't a preacher for our first six months while we were there, and it took some getting used to, but the messages we learned about God made the truths of the Bible become more real when we heard them from many mouths.

Another thing we liked about the church in the West Kootenai was that there didn't seem to be the same generation gap that we saw back east. In Indiana, the young boys and teens kept to themselves, hanging out in the barn until just before the preaching was to start.

The Amish men didn't talk to them much, and they didn't seem to mind. Even within families, *dats* talked to their teen sons about the farm or the animals, but there were few close relationships.

The first time we went to church in Montana, we walked up to the house where church was being held. The Amish men were circled up — and the Amish bachelors and teens were circled up with them. All the men went around and shook hands. Then, when it was time for church to start, the oldest man entered the house first, and all of the men and younger men followed together. The boys went right in after the older men, and instead of the men sitting by age — from the oldest to youngest — the boys sat with their *dats*. This was different than in Indiana. I liked the feeling of my boys sitting next to me.

Part of the reason for this connection between the generations was the Amish bachelors themselves. Most of them were New Order Amish from Ohio, and they were friendly and outgoing, taking an interest in the younger teens. The older men in the Amish community also took an interest in our boys. All of a sudden, our boys were acknowledged by the community. This was different than in Indiana, where you sometimes felt like a face in the crowd. We'd finally found a community with older people who had wisdom to offer our boys.

I found the New Order Amish men refreshing. In our Old Order community in Indiana, the New Order Amish church was frowned upon. They were thought to be too liberal, so much so in fact that the Old Order Amish weren't allowed to have communion with the New Order. Because of this, the Amish bachelors would travel back to their homes for one of the two communion services in the church's yearly calendar. The community seemed quieter when they were gone — more solemn.

In addition to their spiritual openness, the New Order bachelors also gathered together for weekly singings, and they invited anyone from the church to join them. I was amazed how they harmonized while they sang — we'd never heard anything like this before. In Indiana harmonizing was frowned upon, but listening to the music seemed to open up my spiritual side.

The bachelors enjoyed gathering together with the local Amish families too, and we'd often have them over to our house. We greatly enjoyed the fellowship and the singing.

Every year the highlight of the West Kootenai Amish community is the Amish Auction. It had started years before to help raise money for a premature Amish baby who needed extensive medical care and had high hospital bills. Since then, the money was used for the small Amish school. What people may not know is that the Amish never buy insurance. The community is each other's insurance, with hospital bills covered by the community. When someone has a doctor's bill, the cost is broken up and split among all those in the local church district, and if the bill is large, the Amish often get creative on how to raise funds, like the auction.

One year my uncles from Indiana came to visit for the auction. We worked on a log cabin that we were planning on auctioning off. The day before the event, we gathered in that cabin and had a singing party. The harmonizing of the music was beautiful. Clear joy radiated off my uncles' faces. My smile was wide as I realized they were experiencing a glimpse of what our family had found in this Montana community. It hurt my heart though to know they couldn't take it home with them.

CHAPTER 9

Deciding to Stay

ORA JAY

Twelve to fifteen Amish families and twenty to thirty Amish bachelors lived in the West Kootenai. They were there because they wanted a better life for themselves and their children, so some of the standards weren't set so high. We were allowed to have bikes, for instance, as well as power mowers, rubber tires on our buggies, and phones in the shacks on the road — which was a huge thing for us. Yet the people were considered more righteous in dress and action. It was just the type of place we were looking for. In addition, the people there — both Amish and *Englisch* — were friendly to each other, and there was more interaction between them.

We arrived in Montana in May 1990 — just in time to enjoy the summer, which is anticipated all year long. The warm sun cloaks the mountains, rising before five in the morning and setting after ten at night. No one wants to stay inside. After all, snow kept us inside in the winter and rain kept us inside in the spring. The muddy roads dry out in the summer, wildflowers pop up along the edges, wild creatures appear at every turn, and locals find themselves hiking the hills, tending their gardens, and enjoying the lake. Huckleberries ripen in

July, and many women take buckets into the mountains on hikes to pick the ripe berries. Huckleberries are one fruit that cannot be cultivated on farms, so they are a special treat, although we often have to share them with the bears. Flathead cherries are also in season, and Irene enjoyed canning them.

Summer also brought visitors. Hardly a weekend passed when someone wasn't in town. It was wonderful seeing our friends from Indiana, and we had fun showing them around. Many tourists visited the area. As summer warmed the Montana air and more tourists arrived, the peculiar Amish became as much an attraction as the lakes, mountains, hiking trails, and bears. More than once we'd be driving our buggies down the dirt road and someone would stop their car, get out, and snap a picture. I suppose no one ever expected to see Amish in the mountains of Montana — wolves, bears, and elk, yes, but not Amish.

Ministers and their families would come to visit, and we'd invite them to share in the service. Sometimes, if they had to leave before Sunday, we'd have church during the week. In a small community like ours, it was easier to pause on a weekday and have church.

As our first year came to an end, I told Irene that we had to talk about returning. The year had passed quickly, and I was not interested in going back to Indiana. My uncle didn't want us to leave, and he offered me a job for more money than I could make in Indiana. It gave me an excuse to say to Irene, "Look, we can earn more here; we should stay."

Irene submitted to that, though life grew harder for her at that point. When we were planning on only staying one year, we had lots of visitors — friends and family from back east. But when we decided to stay, we knew our world would change. We would have fewer visitors. At the same time, Irene was beginning to see that things didn't always have to be as she thought, as she was raised. Day by day we started to understand a little more about freedom — and about grace. The change was slow, but it came a little at a time, with each Montana sunrise.

IRENE

In April 1991, while still deciding whether we should stay in Montana, we went back to Indiana for a visit. I was in my second trimester, although it is an Amish tradition not to draw attention to one's pregnancy, especially in the early stages. Being in Indiana was harder than I had expected. As we spent time in the familiar community, we didn't seem to fit in as we once had. More than once I found myself thinking, *Well, maybe there's not as much here as I thought.*

Still, the thought of moving to Montana for good was hard. My main concern was my family — my *dat* and siblings. What would they say? I knew they'd be against a permanent move.

They accepted our decision fairly well — until a rumor started circulating that Ora Jay and I were planning to join a New Order church. My family was against that. Although today they'd probably be happy if we had joined a New Order church because at least we'd still be Amish.

On the way back from Indiana I started having contractions, and just as we got off the train in Whitefish I miscarried. Quite traumatic!

Losing the baby was hard, but the prospect of giving up our Indiana community was even harder. After our visit I knew that moving to Montana was the right decision, but it wasn't an easy one. Some days I would sit by myself and cry, "I'm so lonesome for home. I want to go back, but I don't know what I want there."

It was the longest I'd ever been away from my family, and the feelings of depression came and went for about a year. Ora Jay tried to soothe me, but with caring for all our children, I rarely had time to rest. That's when my husband learned to pray as he never had before. Thankfully, God had brought people into our lives to show him how to do that. And I soon discovered that God had many more plans for us in those Montana mountains.

Letter to Family

May 16, 1991

Dear folks,

Greetings in Jesus' name! 'Tis Thursday after dinner and thought I should start my writing task again. To let you know how things are. We came back to Kootenai safe but in a different way than we had expected. The second morning on the train I discovered I was spotting some. Till after noon I started having some contractions. But we just lived on hopes we could make it to Whitefish yet. We did then, but barely. Just as we got off the train I felt it coming.

Beebe was there so he rushed us over to the North Valley Hospital emergency room. There they took care of me and said I have to stay at least overnight. So Ora Jay, David, and the boys went on home. The doctor released me the next day after dinner. So Ora got someone to come and get me. Doctor said that the cord was twice around the neck, which was the cause of the miscarriage so we feel there was probably not one thing that could have been done to prevent it. And we want to accept it as God's will...

This morning Gerald was saying we want to go to Dawdy's. Then I said they are far away. Then he said we can go down the hill and we can just use Lady (the horse)!

There are some visitors here again. Haven't seen any except from the road. Some of Steve Linda's relatives and also Ivan's daughter Betty brought five of her friends along back from Ohio.

Is 9:00 and can't see too well to write anymore. We should not even light a light so we'd go to bed when it's time. But they are playing ball yet, so will have to light one when they come in...

Sheet's full, your turn now.

So long,
Ora Jay's all

Letter to Family

June 26, 1991

Dear folks at home,

Greetings in Jesus' holy name! Wednesday evening about 8:15 and we're sitting here at Alkali Lake waiting on some moose. Lately the people have been seeing them so we decided to try it too. Mary and Lucy saw nine different ones one morning. Ora Jay and Marion went with some others to Eureka to a tool sale (hand tools mostly).

I was at the store today then Leona said just today Daniel Otto and about five of his children came so guess we'll have church on Sunday again. Ora's Lorrie started taking instructions for baptism last Wednesday evening. We had church while Alvin T. Yoders, Christie Y. and Bishop Eli Millers, Bishop Emanuel Troyers (Ohio), and Bishop John Beechy's (Ohio) were here yet. Tuesday we had grös gmā [communion]. Guess they will be depending that there will be enough minister visitors this summer to give Lorrie's instructions [to be baptized]....

This morning we had a surprise when a van drove in. Edward Hostetlers (Hoosier Buggy) got off but stayed only a few minutes. Perry Masts, Andy E. Bontragers, and LeRoy D. Millers were also da-by [with them]. They are on a western trip and will not be here for church tomorrow....

Last week Ora Jay, Danny, LeRoy, and I went up a mountain to a clear cut to hunt mushrooms. That was fun to pick them where they were so many. We had fifteen pounds that time. The Saturday before Ora Jay and two oldest boys had gone and had around twenty pounds. They biked home and had gone up with the girls that went to Lake Geneva. We had hitched up Ginger in a road cart. (We drive him now too and he's chiter [better] than Lady.) It was at least ten miles or more. I canned seven quarts and froze some and we ate a lot!...

So long,
Ora Jay's and all

Letter to Family

Dear Whoever,

Hello, how are you? I'm fine. Today two weeks ago we went mushroom hunting on a mountain northeast of Mt. Robinson. We had to carry our bikes through a woods to get there. When we got out of the woods we had to go a few miles yet before we got there. Just as we started down the road we saw a bear run across the road. We found about a bushel in about two hours. Me and Eli help Dad put up houses. We made one for Delbert Bontrager.

You should tell Ervin's they should come out here.

Well, page is full so I'll stop. See ya later.

From Somebody,
Marion

Letter to Family

August 27, 1991
Nine years ago, a sad night

Dear Mom and Dad,

   Greetings of love in Jesus' name! This is Tuesday evening and Marion is washing dishes. Is 9:00 already and is dark so would be time for bed. We were late tonight as we had our dinner about 3:00 so were not in a hurry for supper! And washed yet after dinner so some is out yet. The boys are supposed to bring the rest in yet, which they are snootzing [grumbling] about.

   The reason we were late for dinner was because we went fishing (of all things!). Ora Jay, Danny and LeRoy and I. We got twelve salmon. On the reservoir ...

   Sounded like Jo Coblentz's are coming out from Hillsboro. So there will be quite an increase in scholars. With Lester Graber's and Noah Yoder's also yet. School will start on Friday. A half day. (Marion's birthday.)

Ora Jay's and all

CHAPTER 10

Englisch in Montana

ORA JAY

The biggest difference between Shipshewana and the West Kootenai was the proximity and connectedness to the *Englisch*. In LaGrange County, Indiana, the Amish stayed separate from the *Englisch*. There was an "us-and-them" mentality. We hadn't planned on befriending any *Englisch* when we moved to Montana, but they were our neighbors. We also saw there was a friendship amongst them unlike what we were used to.

After being in Montana and becoming friends, we soon realized the *Englisch* had higher moral standards than we did — kindness, positive attitudes, a sense of freedom. Talking with new *Englisch* friends, we discovered they were honest about their battles in life, and they supported each other spiritually and physically. This was something we weren't used to back in Indiana. Of course, even though we noticed these things, we weren't interested in leaving the Amish lifestyle. Instead, we were drawn to the openness to spiritual conversations and thought we could improve ourselves and help to improve the Amish community.

I have to admit that even though I had lived most of my life in

Indiana, going back was a culture shock. Everyone seemed more reserved than I remembered. I missed the open conversations about God and the Bible that we had in Montana. I missed the kindness and encouragement that we often got from the *Englisch* there.

It's sad to say, but an outpouring of unconditional love is foreign to the Amish way of thinking. They don't encourage each other in the Lord, and they are more quick to point out a flaw than to bless someone. Maybe it's because that's how they see God — as Someone who looks over their shoulders to make sure they're doing the right thing. Rarely would an Amish person say to another Amish person, "God loves you just the way you are." They would see that statement as false, foreign. They wouldn't say, "God is in you." Instead they would be quick to point out how imperfect they are. They would focus on the things they felt they should be doing instead of what Christ Jesus has already done.

An Amish man would be quick to relate, "God has so much love for us that He gave us His only Son." Yet saying it and believing it are two different things. Taking it into your heart is a different matter completely. I listened with curiosity. Was God not as harsh as I once thought? Was He more interested in me than I could ever imagine?

These were the messages we were hearing from some of our non-Amish friends. Hearing these things and opening our hearts to their love started to break down the wall that our Amish ways had carefully built up over the years.

The truth is, it's easier to follow the rules. Then you don't have to be close with God. You don't have to search your own heart. It's easier to have a set of dos and don'ts than to be Christ centered and continually turning to Him. It's easier to go to church and let someone else encourage you — direct you — instead of going to God, and allowing Him to fill you, so that you can provide encouragement for someone else.

My earliest childhood memories of the *Englisch* were of our neighbors Sam and Pearl Rowan. We often used their phone, and they were nice people. I would go as far as to say they were friends of our family. I had my first experience with television and radio in their home. Sometimes, as kids, when we visited the Rowans' house, they would turn on the television for us. I was so glued to it that I couldn't move. We would never ask them to turn it on, but we'd hint at it. The people and images that came to life on the screen were of a different world, and it's not that we wanted to be part of that world — we were just curious about it. I learned at a young age that even though the world was enticing, letting it draw you away would lead you away from God.

Growing up Amish isn't as simple as it seems. We were well taken care of, well provided for, and we had a place to live, food to eat, and people to be around. We were protected. We weren't abused. But our security was just that — being around family and following the rules. I felt that I needed to please others to be accepted by them.

There was a pecking order within our community. If you were obedient, listened to others, and did as they wanted, you were accepted. If you stepped aside, fingers were pointed, and you weren't accepted. That was our life. That's why you see people doing the same thing — dressing exactly the same, driving the same buggies, doing their yard the same, and doing the wash the same.

There is also a ranking system in Amish communities. There are bullies. There are people who are more popular. As a ten- and eleven-year-old boy, I felt like a face in the crowd. That's a common problem in an Amish community with so many children in large families. I wasn't important, and our family was far from popular. More than anything I wanted to be recognized. Of course, my parents would never encourage me to be "someone." The most important thing was to put others before yourself. Yet I saw that even when everyone was supposed to be caring for everyone else, some got more attention, and others were considered to be "less" in the community.

Maybe I was especially aware of this because my *dat* was not popular. He smoked all his life and wasn't considered very spiritual. To add to the challenges, my *dat* had an extra large lip — it was different from most Amish men. The boys in the community called him *Schnoot* ("big nose"), which hurt me a lot. By comparison, my uncle was a preacher and well liked. How godly your parents seem to the community makes a difference.

I might have been shaken by the ways others treated my family, but I felt loved and cared for by my parents. I don't remember ever getting a hug and kiss — that's not the Amish way — but there was an underlying feeling of love.

I adored my grandpa. I spent as much time with him as with my own family, and my grandparents steered my thoughts even more than my parents. Outside of school I spent my time with my family and went to church every Sunday. I had ten uncles, one of whom was only three years older than I was, and we did all types of hair-raising and dangerous things together.

But on Sundays there was no wildness. We were expected to behave.

When I was eight or nine years old, a preacher talked about hell. I can't remember the man's words, but I remember the fear that overcame me. On the way home, our buggy filled with family members, I asked *Dat*, "What keeps us from going to hell?" *Mem* and *Dat* looked at each other. They were uncomfortable and didn't know what to say. I didn't get an answer. I got the impression that all I needed to do was just follow the rules of the church. Growing up, Irene had the same feeling. She believed that all she could do to avoid hell was to behave as much as possible. It's all she had to hang on to.

Many people don't realize that there is no true hope of salvation in most Amish churches. The concept that faith in Jesus is the only way is not taught. If we wanted to ensure a spot — we had to work for it and live a good Amish life. So as I grew, I just did what I could to fit in. I figured that I'd do all I could do and hope for the best.

IRENE

Before moving to Montana, my understanding of salvation was that if you followed the church rules and did good things, then you would most likely go to heaven. But there wasn't any assurance. We did have the comfort that our girls went to heaven because they were so young when they died. We strived to live a better life and always do good, and we thought that was going to get us there as well. But I didn't know that eternal life actually starts here on earth. That was a new thought to me when I heard it.

Even in Montana, I did my best to stick by the rules because I knew that's what my father wanted. Even though he lived nearly two thousand miles away, his opinion still mattered.

Ora Jay would always test the rules. When we were dating, Ora Jay would talk about getting a car. I never said it directly, but I basically told him that he'd have to choose between me and a car. I knew that's what my *dat* would want. My *dat* wouldn't accept Ora Jay if he got a car.

Once we were married the "had-tos" and "shoulds" followed us, and we did our best to raise our children to be humble and respectful and to work hard. We thought back to how the Bible was shared with us, and we tried to follow suit. Ora Jay's *mem* would read from a Bible storybook, and at times his grandfather would kneel down to pray before he went to bed.

My parents also had a daily ritual of reciting a prayer out of the book, mornings and evenings, and we also did a special Bible reading at Christmas. My *dat* was a good reader, and he encouraged us to read too. He would hand us girls books to read, including Bible stories. He'd also read from a popular prayer book, and he encouraged us to do the same. I did so, but it was written in German, so I only understood a small portion of it.

Ora Jay and I did our best to pass on our beliefs to our children, just as they'd been passed on to us. We'd have a quiet prayer with our children at meal times and recite a prayer out of the prayer book before bed. But still we worried that they wouldn't stay Amish. Our worries lessened in Montana, but they were still there. When some accident would happen to someone who left the Amish community, people would say that it was the result of their rebellion. "I suppose they wish now they'd never left," people would say. There was comfort in knowing you had obeyed the church.

Amish parents often worry about their older children, especially those who are old enough to join the church but haven't. The Amish believe such children have no hope of heaven if they die. An Amish parent's worst nightmare is that one of their sons or daughters will die in a car accident while being "wild." They'd go to hell for certain.

That's how we saw God during most of our growing-up years. He was someone who always watched to make sure we followed the rules. In fact, Ora Jay's parents, who referred to God as *Gut Mon* (Good Man), would say things like, "*Gut Mon* is watching you" ... "*Gut Mon* doesn't want you to do this ..." Whether it was sneaking cigarettes, telling a fib, being dishonest, or watching television —

"*Gut Mon* knows." To Ora Jay, *Gut Mon* knew everything, and nothing could be hidden from Him.

Before moving to the West Kootenai, prayer meant saying the Lord's Prayer in German, silently in our minds. As children sometimes we'd just count instead because we knew exactly how long it took. But as we spent time with *Englisch* friends in the West Kootenai area, they talked about prayer differently. They acted as if one could talk directly to God, and He cared. They said their prayers *out loud*.

If my father had heard me praying that way, he would have said, "Do you think you can pray better than the prayer book? You're arrogant to think that."

Yet even though everything within me told me that the Amish way was right, I was drawn into relationships with non-Amish friends that opened my eyes to a whole new approach to God. First, I noticed their compassion. People already knew about the girls when we got to Montana — Amish and *Englisch* alike. Everywhere we went, we were known as the family who had lost our daughters.

The non-Amish were concerned about our loss. They wanted to know more about it and how we were doing. We could see they cared for us, and we found ourselves opening up in ways we hadn't since the accident. While our Amish friends were mostly silent about our loss — and didn't know what to say — our new non-Amish friends wanted to know what was in our hearts. We sensed they had something different, something that we didn't have, yet that didn't make sense to us. Didn't we Amish have the right way?

CHAPTER 11

Changes Within

ORA JAY

One Amish family in the West Kootenai had what they called "family night," and they invited us to join them. John and Kathryn Miller, along with their married children and their families, would get together to read the Scriptures and pray. This was the first time we had heard an Amish family — adults and grown children — praying out loud together, and not out of a prayer book but out of their mouths, from their hearts. In fact we'd never heard any Amish person pray out loud from the heart before, not even the preachers. Even though we sometimes did a devotion in the morning with our children, having a family night was different than anything we'd experienced. And we thought that was good.

A group of us also started having church every week instead of every two weeks. We called the "off" week Sunday school, but there were some who were against it. "You might learn too much about the Bible," some in the Amish community would say. To know too much was to focus on one's self — to become prideful. "If you meet every week, you're leaving tradition. And when you leave to try something else, watch out. Soon you'll stop being Amish." We had no choice but to keep unity within our church, so we stopped the Sunday school gatherings on the off weeks.

While our Amish friends were discouraging change, our *Englisch* friends were encouraging us to open our hearts and talk about things we'd never discussed before. One of our *Englisch* friends even asked me if I ever felt guilty about the accident. I'd been awake one minute before the semi-truck hit us and had fallen asleep again. I finally admitted that I did feel guilty for a time — Irene and I both did. Irene never blamed me because she'd been asleep too.

Of course, you can't change a mistake, and you can never rewind the clock and take your life back to the way it was before, but through those conversations with our new friends, God brought healing from the guilt. Since then, we've chosen to enjoy being with the people whom God has granted us to be with at this moment.

We also talked about how God allowed the timing of that semi-truck down the road. One or two minutes' difference and we would still have our girls. In a way it felt good talking about these things with our *Englisch* friends. We realized they cared.

I also remember the first time I prayed out loud. It was at David Pereslete's place. He had invited me and another Amish man to visit, and he talked to us about God. I sat there and listened, amazed by the peace and joy I saw in him. He encouraged me to pray. Something inside told me that I had to do this, that God had something more for me. I kneeled and put my face to the floor.

I don't remember what I said, though I'm sure it wasn't eloquent. Still, it was the first time I'd ever heard my own voice utter a prayer to God. When I left David's place, I had a new sense of freedom. I had spilled my thoughts to the Lord. And even though my upbringing rejected that kind of prayer, I wondered, *How can it be wrong?*

The *Englischers* also invited us to prayer meetings. We went because the people were friendly, and we could tell they cared about us. Despite our criticisms of the *Englisch* lifestyle, how they raised their children, and the way they dressed, we were drawn to their kindred spirit that we are all children of God.

So Irene, the older boys, and I would go to these prayer meetings, and the owners of the home came to greet us. They would introduce us to everyone, and we were given welcoming hugs. This was new to us. No one hugged in the Amish church, and it was awkward at first. In fact, the first time I ever received a hug by anyone other than my wife was at a prayer meeting. But we were polite and accepted them. We soon came to appreciate them.

IRENE

As a teenager, I used to babysit for an *Englisch* pastor in LaGrange. I would watch his family closely, and I was fascinated by the hugs they gave each other when family or friends came over. I hadn't experienced that growing up. I don't remember receiving hugs from my parents or any other adults. I was always confused when the Amish preachers shared the story of the prodigal son, whose father hugged him when he returned, or the story of Jacob and Esau, who gave each other a hug and a kiss after being a long time apart. I'd think, *Why don't we do that?* There's never an occasion for an Amish man to hug or kiss a family member out of affection. Kisses are used only to show church unity. That's just the way things were done.

ORA JAY

In Montana I learned so much about true friendship and how to have an open-hearted relationship with God through prayer and Scripture. I had also been impressed by the relationships our non-Amish friends had with their children. Watching them, their love for each other and the community, made an impact. I asked one *Englisch* man about it, and he invited Irene and me over to listen to some messages on cassette tapes. At first, Irene and I almost couldn't sit in that chair. Listening to anything on a cassette player was completely forbidden, yet the messages were so convicting and so inspiring. They helped us with our parenting so much that we couldn't say, "This is wrong." We also learned about the role of a husband, the role of a wife, and how to have a godly home.

We also began listening to A. W. Tozer tapes. His preaching was like nothing we had heard before. He quoted Scriptures in English, which was easier to understand than German. We got far more out of those cassette tapes than we had gotten our whole lives from the Amish church. We were encouraged to seek God for ourselves and listen to His voice.

When we went back east to Indiana to visit family, we missed the openness that we felt in the West Kootenai. We missed the open conversations, the Bible readings, and the prayer times. We missed the encouragement in our parenting. We even missed the hugs.

In Indiana, I remember talking to a family member about how God had been changing us and leading us.

"You think God is leading you?" he asked, puzzled.

"*Ja*, I do. He is."

The man shook his head as if that was the craziest thing he'd ever heard.

"What about you? Why don't you seek Him in that way? God wants to lead you too." Tension tightened my chest because I knew my very question probably sounded disrespectful. Still, I had to ask. "Why not give Him a chance?" I thought of a verse from Malachi (3:10), so I shared it with my relative, " 'Bring the whole tithe into the storehouse, that there may be food in my house. Test me in this,' says the LORD Almighty, 'and see if I will not throw open the flood-gates of heaven and pour out so much blessing that there will not be room enough to store it.' If God does this when we give Him our tithe, how much more He will open the floodgates of heaven when we give Him our whole hearts!"

"You're just talking out of your gut," he told me.

"The Bible actually says that."

He stroked his beard and shook his head again. "You're Bible-wise. You're too wise."

My heart ached because my words couldn't penetrate his heart. Even sadder, God's words couldn't penetrate it either.

After a short visit to Indiana, we were eager to return to the West Kootenai, but when we did, we were told that the Millers had stopped having their family nights of singing, praying, and reading the Bible because the church had discouraged them. "No family nights?" Irene said, her eyes wide. "They're taking that away from us too, just like Sunday school?"

It got us thinking, *What's wrong with this?* Why should a church discourage people from reading the Bible and praying together? Even when we asked each other that, we knew the answer. Bible reading was for preachers. To read too much was to make one "wise in their own eyes" — "Bible-wise," as my relative had said. And prayer was taking pride in your own words. Yet that taste of reading God's Word wasn't something we could shake.

Our hopes were crushed. We'd been excited about the changes we'd seen within our Amish church and with our Amish friends. We'd grown spiritually and had seen our friends doing the same. We were hoping to turn our traditional Amish church into a spiritual Amish church. Now it was clear that that wasn't going to happen easily.

"Irene, I wonder if this isn't the place to be after all," I said. We knew that we would never go back to Indiana, but if we left the West Kootenai, where could we go?

We talked about going to Libby, Montana, just sixty miles away, at the bottom edge of Lake Koocanusa. Some of our spiritual Amish friends had moved there and were starting their own church. Later, some of John Miller's family started a new settlement in St. Ignatius.

"Maybe we should go to St. Ignatius," Irene told me one night. Her voice was shaking and tears streaked her cheeks. "I hear it's so much more spiritual. I'm tired of fighting the carnal people in the West Kootenai."

"Is that what we *should* do?" I asked her.

Irene turned away. "That's what I want to do."

"*Ja*, and what then? Then we can cling to some of the Amish stuff and be accepted a little, but deep down we know that isn't the answer."

But what was the answer? Walking away from all we grew up with — from those we love — didn't seem to be the answer either.

Circle Letter, Grieving Parents Group

January 26, 1992

Dear friends,

Greetings in Jesus' holy name! This is Sunday evening. And we are just at home. It doesn't happen very often as most times we go back to the singing which we also enjoy. We're in Sunday school today, then this afternoon we went to visit Dave Kauffman's Jr. He came home from the hospital after being there since the day before New Year's. He had an accident while on a logging job when he got hit in the head by a log. He was unconscious for a week and has improved quite rapidly but is still not alright. The right side of his face doesn't function right yet, but doctor feels it will come back with time. . . .

For the time being we will stay here. We have no definite plans yet. We are planning on going "East" again for a visit in March, Lord willing! "Let us pray for each other not faint by the way in this sad world of sorrow and care."

Just us,
Ora Jay, Irene, and all

CHAPTER 12

Discovering Truth

ORA JAY

Having Bibles written in High German is something the Amish have held on to in order to maintain their culture. It's a tradition. Both Irene and I learned some High German in school, but since most Amish don't know High German well, the meaning of the Scripture is only guessed at as it's preached about. We learn a little from the preaching. Sometimes we think we know what part of a Scripture verse means, but we often don't know what the other half means or we think it means something that it doesn't. And that's where doctrine comes in. It's explained to us, and we think it has to be a certain way because we don't understand it, so how it's explained has to be right.

Finally I decided to read the Bible in English so I could expound on it when we talked about the Scriptures. We found a Bible with English on one side and German on the other, and this helped immensely. As Irene and I started reading, some words jumped out at us. They spoke to our spirits and confirmed what God had been saying to our hearts — that there is something more to a relationship with Him than we'd been taught. Then we started comparing the

German and the English, comparing some of these sayings that were going around in our Amish traditions and beliefs. "Ah, this Scripture doesn't mean what we thought it meant," we told each other. We learned the truth, and as it went into our hearts and changed our lives, it confirmed that it was okay — *okay* — to know God and to do what He asks us to do.

Even as our eyes were opened, change came slowly over time. Our Amish traditions were deeply ingrained, including the belief that it was by our *works* that we are saved. But as we read, we saw a little spark of grace. The Word of God came alive, almost as if God was tapping us on the shoulder and saying, "Take a look at *this*."

We had been taught that we needed to obey our parents, as the Bible teaches. But as Irene and I studied the Scriptures, we learned that the word *obey*, as well as the phrase *honor your parents*, doesn't mean "take orders from them," but it means to love and care for them, to not cast them out as if they were nothing.

We had also been taught that there could be no grace for us unless we kept the vows we made on our bended knees when we joined the Amish church. But Scripture teaches that vows should not be made to a church or to a body of people or to a belief system. Vows should be made only to God. And we will never leave those vows that we made to God.

One might think that discovering the good news of Jesus was refreshing to us — and it was in many ways. The problem was that the more truth we discovered, the more we questioned our place in the Amish community. Many times we went to bed praying, crying, and lamenting. It was a great struggle, yet through our brokenness, we were being strengthened in the Lord. God had more in store for us — on heaven and on earth — than we could ever imagine.

God also showed us a new freedom when we started praying with our non-Amish neighbors. According to the Amish, if you associate with the non-Amish, you could not be a member of the church. You could associate in some ways — like work — but not in Bible study and prayer.

Word got back to Indiana about how we were starting to question things. First someone wrote, "We hear that you are not content with the Amish church," and then they'd tell us how we should be content. Our family in Indiana would send us verses to remind us of the traditions we'd been taught, and we'd take those verses and look them up, because we really wanted to know what the Bible was saying. Reading the larger context of those verses, we would discover that they really didn't mean what the Amish thought they meant. It just confirmed in our hearts what God was saying.

As God's Word grew clearer, we found more freedom.

IRENE

By 1992 we had decided that we belonged in Montana for good. We were growing closer to God day by day, and we had many questions about the Amish way of life, mostly about the numerous traditions we'd taken for granted for so many years.

In April of that year Ora Jay and I went back east again for a month to get ready to sell a lot of our personal belongings by auction, and also to sell the farm that we'd been renting out to a young married couple.

Standing in my farmhouse again, I felt as if it were someplace I had once been in a dream. Everything was so familiar yet so different too. Sun flowed through the open window, warming me. But still, I crossed my arms over my chest, pulling them close. A chill raced up my back at the realization of what we were doing, what we were leaving.

Looking out the kitchen window, I saw Ora Jay showing an Amish man around. Would he be one of those bidding on our place? Ora Jay pointed to the row of trees just behind the house. We'd planted them when they were just saplings, and now they were nearly as tall as the house. Although the trees had grown taller, nearly everything else had stayed the same in the last two years. Our renters had cared for it well. Now we would be leaving so many things we had worked so hard to build and trusting them to another man.

A warm breeze carried the boys' laughter through the open window. My heartbeat quickened as I remembered the girls laughing in such a way. I placed a hand on my heart, realizing that almost ten years had passed since we lost them. I closed my eyes, trying to picture them, remember them. If they had lived, they'd be old enough now to be thinking about marriage. And — I bit my lip — maybe there would be grandchildren in several years.

I placed my hand on my growing belly, realizing that I still had many years before I'd be a grandmother. I was excited and nervous about the new little one on the way. After two miscarriages I was hoping for a healthy baby in a few months. I didn't dare hope for a girl.

I turned from the window and glanced at the two piles I'd started in the living room: one pile of things to auction off; another pile of things to keep. The auction pile was much bigger.

It's a new life, a new start, I reminded myself.

I walked to the pantry to sort through more things, and I noticed Suetta's and Sarah Mae's names on the inside of the door. There we had marked our children's year heights with dates. It was just one more thing we'd be leaving behind. One more memory.

Days and weeks passed, and soon we'd gathered together all the furniture and things that we wanted to move to Montana. We had good friends, Brian Turney and his wife, who'd offered to drive a U-Haul truck full of all the items we wanted to keep. Still, we couldn't afford to bring much.

We spent over a month going through everything, deciding what to sell and what to keep. Even though it was hard to get rid of things, we had made up our minds that our life was to change and the priority was to do better for our children. That meant we needed to sell the things that kept us looking back. It was a relief to sell some of the things. But it was hard to see all the things that we'd worked so hard for being sold — and at cheap prices. We'd just tell ourselves over and over that God had bigger and better plans. Somehow that helped us stick with our decision. A few special things were hardest to sell, like the buggy that Ora Jay had made by himself when he was a teenager, our horses, and my furniture.

The auctioneer had told us that everything could be sold in one evening, though it stretched well into the night. As the sky darkened, we went for lanterns so that we could finish the auction. Part of me couldn't believe this was happening. Another part of me was thankful for it.

ORA JAY

I'll never forget the night of the auction. We watched most of our worldly possessions being packed up and hauled away by strangers and friends. Mostly I tried to stay out of the way so I wouldn't see stuff going. The hardest was seeing the farm go — the place we raised our girls, where our memories of them were.

It was also painful because the people around us didn't understand why we were doing this. Why were we selling our things for little money and giving up our beautiful farm to live in a wild place? It was as if we were telling our old friends we had found something better and no longer valued their friendship. That's how it seemed to them.

Nobody talked to us about it, of course, but we overheard them. When they talked to us, they mostly just avoided the subject. We felt very alone.

I couldn't wait for things to end so Irene and I could talk alone. It was difficult to see all our hard work being sold, but I reminded myself that making a move for the better took priority.

As we headed back to Montana it was as if we were truly starting over, and it wasn't a comfortable feeling. Even now when we visit Indiana I get a twinge in my heart to see the old place. There is a new, young family living in our home, and it's good to see life within those walls. But it's also good to remember, to see the handprints in the cement and how tall the trees we planted have grown.

Leaving everything was harder on Irene. Back in Montana, she faced a depression that she couldn't shake. Many nights she couldn't sleep and found herself crying. Many, many nights she'd slip outside and go into a shed to cry so that no one would hear her wails.

She — more than I — saw what was coming. She knew that if we continued heading down this path, we would leave the Amish. And even as we considered what to do, God gave us a wonderful gift … one we cherished. One that told us He was looking down on us, watching over us.

Circle Letter, Grieving Parents Group

May 11, 1992

Dear friends around the circle,
Greetings in Jesus' high and holy name!…

Last Friday we got some baby calves — thirty of 'em. Boy, it sure keeps one on the lookout to keep 'em all alive. One died already and some more got sick. We had been having very dry and warm weather till just the last couple days, which is not the best for the calves. Yesterday it rained off and on. We had been wishing for rain for quite some time, and now we got it when the calves came, which we would have preferred not to have right at this time.…

We went to Indiana for a visit, which ended up being longer than we intended — were gone seven weeks. We sold our farm and had a public auction one evening for some personal property too. Now this week the rest of our belongings will arrive here — Lord willing. Sorry we didn't get to see many of you Indiana folks.

So long,
The Eash Family,
Ora Jay and Irene

CHAPTER 13

All We Knew

IRENE

After two miscarriages I was nervous about being pregnant again, but when we returned to Montana, a baby girl was born on July 7, 1992. We named her Saretta after the two girls we lost. I'd been scheduled for a C-section, but I went into labor the evening before, so I had her the natural way. Praise the Lord! And she was a girl! I cried for joy. The Lord was already becoming more real to us, and I thanked Him again and again for her life.

Our new daughter was a gift to our growing family, but we were growing spiritually too. We continued to attend the Amish church, and on the outside nothing changed. But inside . . . we were changing. Slowly how we lived — what we'd known all our lives — didn't seem to fit.

We'd grown up in the Amish church, and that was an important part of our lives. Ora Jay remembers being three or four years old and sitting with his *dat* and putting his head on his lap to sleep. This only works for so long, however, because there are certain rituals in an Amish service that involve standing for Scripture reading, sitting for singing and to listen to the message, and kneeling to pray. A child can't get comfortable for too long.

When I was a child, my favorite part of the service was the snack. A typical service lasts three hours, which is a long time for little ones to sit, so in the middle of the service, cookies and pretzels were passed around to the younger children. Sometimes there were home-made cookies. Other times saltine crackers. Sometimes I would put a saltine cracker around a cookie, eat around the cracker until they were the same shape, then eat the cookie and cracker together.

My *mem* would often bring hankies for the pretzels. She'd tie little knots on the corners to make bowls and then place them on our laps. Ora Jay's *dat* would simply grab a handful of pretzels and hold them in his hand, and Ora Jay would take them out one by one.

This was only for the younger kids, of course, and by age seven or eight (around the time one started school), the child would stop taking a snack. By age nine or ten the child was old enough to sit with friends, instead of a parent. They couldn't act up, though, because every eye in the place was on them, and any inappropriate behavior would be punished. Once I became a mother, I knew it was import-ant to have children sit, listen, and obey. People judged each other by how the kids performed.

Amish church is held in the home, and all Amish homes are built with this in mind. Benches, which are made of wood without backs, are moved from house to house in a bench wagon. They are set up in the house, and the women sit on the kitchen side and the men on the living room side. The preacher stands and preaches in the doorway. A young person is allowed to go out to use the restroom or take a break, but when that happens everyone knows about it.

Since most Amish communities have four preachers, the preachers that aren't preaching that day sit on a bench against one wall. The visiting preachers or bishops sit there too. The Amish are seated from oldest to youngest, with the oldest sitting in the back of the room. This means that the boys who are old enough to sit on their own sit right across from the preachers. Talk about intimidating!

The preacher shares the message with neither notes nor a Bible in hand. Sometimes he has a verse to share, but mostly a story. A lot of the stories come from the Amish-Mennonite magazine *Family Life*.

The break time for children comes after the first part of prayer. Everyone stands up for the Scripture reading, and then, the boys go to the barn. It is considered less of a disturbance for the boys to leave to stretch their legs for a bit while everyone is standing. In our church it became an expected tradition, especially since the boys couldn't understand the German reading anyway. They knew how to time things so they'd be back before the preacher was done reading the Scripture.

Growing up, we knew what to expect from church, and we were expected to be there. It was not optional. Ora Jay remembers waking up and feeling sick some mornings. His *dat* would look at him and say, "Go puke. Now let's go to church."

Communion services, which were longer than regular services, were held twice a year and lasted all day. The preachers took turns going through all the Old Testament stories, all in German. Some of the preachers were quite dramatic and held the crowd's attention, while some had monotones and others chanted. Some got very excited, swung their arms, and belted out the stories. Very few just talked.

We had our favorite preachers from our district and other districts too. That was one reason why the Amish have church every other Sunday — so preachers could go back and forth to help each other out.

A few of the preachers could hardly get anything said. They were nervous and cleared their throats often. Remember, you don't have a choice about becoming a preacher or about who will preach. When a preacher goes to church, he doesn't know if he's going to preach that day or not — it all depends on who hasn't preached in a while.

When the youth were ready to join the church, they had to attend nine church services and the preachers would walk them through the Amish Articles of Faith. These articles were also in German, and so the preacher would have to explain them. This would happen away from the main service, in a barn or another room. Baptisms happened twice a year, and those were exciting times. It meant that young people were choosing to join the Amish church, and their parents sighed in relief.

Before baptism, a young man would wear a coat without a flap in the back. Once they were baptized and considered a member of the church, they got a new coat, called a *mutza*, with a slot in the back that overlapped.

Many times I'd hear people say, "You can tell if they're Christians or not by the clothes they wear." When someone said that, they were talking about the Plain clothes they were wearing. To be baptized into the church is the same as being a Christian in the eyes of the Amish. We knew this because it was all we knew. And stepping outside of it was a scary thing.

ORA JAY

About a dozen Amish families lived in the West Kootenai, as well as a few *Englisch* families who considered becoming Amish. Personally, I thought this was spectacular. It seemed good to me that they'd be willing to give up the things of the world to join us. One couple sold their car and only used a horse and buggy. A few families started dressing in the Plain way and attending Amish church.

The only problem was that in the Amish church Scripture is read in High German, and the sermons are preached in Pennsylvania Dutch. The new *Englisch* attendees could understand neither. "How can we use German only with these guys sitting here? They can't understand," I'd ask some of the other church members. Some members thought we should start preaching in English, but others did not want to leave the traditions we knew.

At that time, three elders from our congregation had the job of looking after the church. They were the sticklers. They had an obligation. They couldn't really make a decision about preaching in English on their own, because these men knew they'd be the ones answering to people back east. And even though we were far away in the Montana wilderness, the law of the Amish church had followed us. If a minister or bishop from back east came to reprimand someone, the elders would be the first ones. The elders had to look at the church's rules to consider their decision. Of course, the rules didn't allow preaching or Scripture reading in English, and soon our *Englisch* friends no longer attended.

My heart was crushed. Since I was starting to read the Bible for myself, I began to question where the Amish laws came from. God's Word showed us that we had more freedom in Christ than what we'd been taught. In the Amish church we'd been raised to believe we only needed to listen and to follow our leaders in order to be good and to appease God. But we were starting to see that instead of just listening to our leaders, it was our responsibility to read and learn God's Word to learn right and wrong.

The more we followed Jesus, even that changed. Soon we began to read not only to find the "rules" but also to grow closer to Jesus and seek Him to fill us with the most important virtue of all — love for God and for people. We had discovered it wasn't our buggy or *kapp* that pleased God, but our hearts. And we were being changed from the inside out.

We also were being invited by *Englisch* friends to step out — to try their church and discover the freedom they felt they had in Christ. Of course, what was freedom to them was terrifying to us. In a small community like the West Kootenai we'd be missed in the Amish church, and it wouldn't take long for those in the community to discover where we'd been. And just as the news of our daughters' death had found its way to Montana long before our arrival, the news of our "disobedience" in attending an *Englisch* church would no doubt make it back to Indiana before a week passed. And that news would break our family's hearts even more than our moving had. Maybe even more than the news of our daughters' deaths had.

Circle Letter, Grieving Parents Group

September 15, 1992

Dear circle friends,

Greetings in Jesus' high and holy name!… First I want to thank everyone that gave us meals, bed, etc. We sure enjoyed our visit with you all. And yes, we had a safe trip home and also a nice visit for a couple days in Indiana. Sure spites us to miss the ones that were not able to be there.

To you others that we didn't see, don't know if you found out that we were blessed with one of God's wonderful gifts — a baby girl, Saretta! Eight pounds four ounces at birth on July 7. It was of course a real joy that it's a girl again, and the boys were tickled too, but we do feel unworthy of such a blessing. I went to the doctor for a belated six-week checkup last week and he thought Saretta was growing fine.

We had frost already so garden things are past except digging the potatoes. I saw the mountains have some fresh snow again, so guess that's why it's getting so cool again. But we expect a lot of nice fall weather yet ...

> Till next round,
> Ora Jay, Irene, and all

CHAPTER 14

Attending an Englisch Church

ORA JAY

As we waited on the driveway, I hoped that none of our Amish friends would drive by in their buggies on their way to church and spot us. Our friend's van pulled up, and we all climbed in. The children scrambled into the back, where our friends had laid down the third seat, and a dozen or more children were packed in. Irene and I sat side by side. She wore her *kapp*, and I still wore my hat.

The first time we attended a non-Amish church, Irene felt it was too worldly. There were musical instruments. The people didn't dress Plain, and no one acted as humble as we thought they should. I don't remember much of the message because I was so concerned about the people around me. Our whole lives we'd been taught to dress Plain and to act humble. Even though I'd never say anything, I wondered how these people could call themselves followers of God. Looking back, we now wonder what the community church members thought of Irene and me showing up in our Amish clothes.

On the outside, Irene and I appeared like any other Amish couple. I still wore my beard, but no mustache. But something was changing inside. After a while I let my mustache grow in and I trimmed my beard. My Amish friends were horrified. They could tell we were getting farther and farther from their ways. Many of them didn't realize that the tradition of not wearing a mustache didn't start until World War II, when the mustache was connected with military service. So many of my Amish family and friends think tradition is connected to spiritual things.

Soon letters started arriving from relatives back east: "We hear this . . . we hear that." People from the church visited to talk to us too. They sat down, uneasy, and the reprimands came. "You're not doing what you were taught." Their words struck my heart.

Everyone was watching us, judging us, but no one was listening to our hearts. We knew that if you acted friendly and dressed Plain you'd be approved of. It had been ingrained in us that how you present yourself is how your heart is. It seemed that if we kept our outside appearance looking good, then all would be fine.

We wanted to be accepted by our peers, and so we did our best to do what we should to gain their approval. We attended the Amish church and listened. But the biggest struggle was listening to the sermon. Every time someone would start talking about the rules, following our ancestors, or anything like that, we felt as if spiritual bondage was being placed upon the shoulders of those in our community.

When Amish friends stopped by, we would talk about gardens, and logging, and the weather, but I could tell they were uneasy, though I acted as if I didn't notice. Then, at the last minute before they left, the words of reprimand would come. "You know, you are part of this community. What are we going to do without you?" One minute they pleaded for our friendship. But the next moment the words were more heated. "Don't you know how wrong you are for visiting an *Englisch* church?"

Yes, we knew that according to the Amish church we were wrong, but the changes we were making were because God was speaking to our hearts. Irene and I had made it a goal to be better people.

IRENE

Fall of 1993 brought big changes. First, we purchased forty acres on Deer Path Lane from John Miller, with plans to start building a house in the spring. Also, it was hunting season — something that Ora Jay and the boys looked forward to — but that was the last thing on our minds. Our problems within our Amish community had grown not only because of our choice to build friendships with non-Amish friends but because of the relationships we built with those who seemed radical within the Amish church.

Close friends of ours, Joe and Rachel Coblentz, had planned to rent a house, but at the last minute, doors closed to them. This large family, with twelve children, had no place to go, and so they moved in with us for a time. We had seven children too! Two big families under one roof.

Saretta's crib was set up in the far corner of the living room — the only place for it with twenty-three people in the house. When Saretta made the smallest of squeaks, a flurry of arms, feet, and legs started. Her brothers raced to her crib, trying to be the first to pick her up. With quickened steps the winning boy hurried to me and plopped Saretta down on my lap. She snuggled against my chest and rubbed her eyes, trying to wake up. If ever a baby was welcomed and loved it was Saretta.

Joe and Rachel had made plans to move up from Libby, Montana, to a rental house owned by one of the Amish couples, but only that day they found out they couldn't, because they would not promise not to have cars or *Englisch* people coming to their house. Joe and Rachel didn't feel they could promise that, as they had lots of *Englisch* friends. Also, Joe had gotten into trouble with an Amish church in Wisconsin because he'd preached a sermon there, and the leaders of the church felt he'd preached wrong, yet Joe refused to go back and make peace with them. He didn't want to repent because he didn't think the message that he shared with them was wrong.

One might imagine it would be hard to have that many people — that many children — all under one roof. Our friends had left the community for another Amish church and wanted to come back. We expected that we would be the good examples, but it was the other way around. Their love for each other was evident, and a hunger grew within us for what they had.

The family stayed with us for seven weeks, and it was a joy. We prayed together, sang together, and ate together. Their family was very respectful, and we took note of that.

Lois is the daughter of Joe and Rachel Coblentz. She recently sent us a letter with her memories of the time her family spent with us.

Letter from Lois

August 2013

Hello, Ora Jay and Irene,

My mom called and told me to come up with all the memories I can of when we were staying with you. Well, I'm sure you can guess where my mind was these last few days. It was lots of fun reminiscing, just recalling the atmosphere! I think life for me at that time was about as easy as any time!

We were almost twenty children, crowded into one house. Seems like everyone was fairly good-natured and easy-going, and I do not recall friction. I noticed Irene seemed to have much patience with her hyper, rambunctious little boys, especially Gerald! She was calm and "unflustered" with him, even when he and Keturah were having a blast, jumping on the couches.

We girls were fascinated when Irene decorated Danny's birthday cake (eleventh?). She didn't use special tips, just a big syringe to decorate a regular, iced cake into something "simply" extraordinary and personal.

Prayer meetings were great. Everyone was cheerful. I don't recall peer pressure, and we prayed for anything and everything we could think of that we thought was worth praying for, especially all those "Amish situations" we knew of and talked about!

During this time I was first introduced to the Godly Home Series, by Denny Kenastan. They were a little scary because I was afraid my parents would start following the principles Denny endorsed, and it would have been almost too much for this big sixteen-year-old-going-on-seventeen. I was afraid I'd have to reveal all my little "secrets"!

Some of the things I recall are vague and kind of jumbled. Things that we might have done after we moved away, such as going skating together. I do not recall that the boys and we girls ever flirted with each other, though. The boys were very respectful and respectable and we were never put in an awkward position where I felt self-conscious. Our parents trusted us pretty far too.

And, last of all, this is all from my point of view/opinion. If there was something "questionable" going on or friction, I was oblivious to it! I've got to get back to my schoolchildren. Thanks for all the little gems you allowed me to treasure.

> *God's blessings on all you out West*
> *in your corner of the world,*
> *Lois and Family*

ORA JAY

Of course having this family in our home was not something our local Amish community approved of. People came by to try to talk us out of our actions, to warn us of our disobedience in fellowshipping with those who'd left the Amish church. As expected, letters also came from back east, from concerned family members and friends. "Another family has moved in with you? What good could come out of that?"

When we didn't listen, the church got involved. Three elders showed up at our door. We sat in our yard. They asked what was happening, and I couldn't keep quiet. "God is doing wonderful things in our lives. Irene and I feel closer to Him than we ever have. We've been reading God's Word, and the words seem as if they are alive on the page." I shared some of the Scripture verses and truths we were discovering. Then I focused my gaze on the men. "What about you? Where's your life with God?" None of them answered. Maybe they didn't know what to say.

I couldn't sleep at night. I prayed and asked God to open the hearts of those in our church. I wanted to turn our local Amish community into a spiritual Amish community. We still hadn't seriously considered leaving the Amish. Instead, I thought we could continue to live by the traditions we'd been taught but also open our hearts to God more and more. Yet the elders didn't want to consider any changes. We asked if we could again start a Sunday school for the children, and they refused. We asked if we could meet together for prayer meetings, and they refused that too.

So instead we continued to go to prayer meetings with our *Englisch* friends. We met at the house of an *Englisch* couple, and the living room was so full that some had to sit on the floor. Some got tired and sprawled out on the floor. There were men and women on their knees, worshiping God and lifting up their prayers to Him. Some of the men would lie flat on the floor in a submissive manner. We'd never seen men and women humbling themselves before God in such a way.

Yet we still weren't comfortable letting our Amish friends know that we were attending *Englisch* prayer meetings, so we'd often sneak out. During winter nights, we'd wait until it was dark, hitch up the buggy, and then drive to prayer meetings. Once our horse got spooked and darted off the road into the woods! It was quite a wild ride. When the horse ran between two trees, the buggy got stuck. The horse broke loose from the buggy and ran off, trailing his harness. Before we could jump down, the buggy tipped and spilled us forward onto the ground. Thankfully everything was all right, but we had a lot of explaining to do the next day as to how our buggy got stuck between two trees in the woods!

More letters came, and word had it that we'd joined the New Order Amish. Irene's dad wrote letters: "You don't want to be New Order." Years later when we decided not to be Amish anymore their words changed. "At least you can be New Order," they'd tell us. "It's better than going all the way into the world."

When Joe lived with us, I grew in my faith. I not only began to understand God's Word better, but I wanted to live it out. Joe and I would talk about the Bible, and then we'd pray about who God wanted us to share His good news with that day. God would always bring someone to mind. Then Joe and I would walk down the road and pay various neighbors a visit. We'd go to share God's Word and pray with them. I felt like one of Jesus' disciples.

Too much was happening with the members of the Amish church, so they sent for a bishop from Indiana to come and straighten things out. Joe and Rachel soon moved away to Michigan, and Irene and I felt alone. How could everything be stripped away like that? Where was our support? Irene and I just bawled. "Now there's even less of a chance of making it a spiritual church," we'd say.

It was during that time that I felt God speaking deep in my heart: "You can make it on your own. You don't need others ... you just need Me." I have to say I had a hard time believing that.

Letters from that time show the change happening within us. We were beginning to understand the grace that God provided for us. We now saw that faith in Jesus was enough. When we sat down to write letters, we'd think and pray about what to say. We were certain that our family members and friends wouldn't listen to our explanations, but we hoped they'd listen to the Word of God, so we began to include many Scripture passages. We began to be bold — maybe too bold — but we desperately wanted those we loved to understand the true riches we were finding in an intimate relationship with Jesus Christ. As time went on we got more light from the truth, and our messages changed as we were transformed.

Circle Letter, Grieving Parents Group

September 1, 1993

Dear friends,

Greetings in our Lord Jesus' name! "That My joy might remain in you, and that your joy might be full" (John 15:11 NKJV). If we delight in doing our Father's will, then we can have joy to the fullest. One of our hindrances is thinking about our circumstances, which is one of my weak spots — not putting my full trust in God....

The canning rush has somewhat slowed down, but there's still some to do. Red beets, some more peaches, maybe pears, and tomatoes yet. I have canned more quarts this year than ever before. But of course, the family is growing too.

This is the first week of school — with four scholars again. One out now. He turned fifteen on Monday. Then we have a first grader again. Our thoughts went back to eleven years ago. (The 27th. It was on a Friday too.) We had a first grader for four days, then suddenly her school days were over and her sister did not have to go at all. God planned to take them to a "Better Home." Would sure be different to have sixteen- and eighteen-year-old girls around to help with the work, etc. But that is not our greatest desire — to have 'em here to work. We wanted them to get to heaven, and God called them sooner than we had expected ...

Ora Jay and Irene

Letter to Family

November 11, 1993

Dear siblings,

Greetings to you all in the name of our Lord Jesus. "And whatsoever you do in word or deed, do all in the name of the Lord Jesus, giving thanks to God the Father through Him" (Colossians 3:17 NKJV).

I guess this verse kinda struck me the first time I read it. I had to think how many things do I do that my mind does not even go to God? Or even some little things we are prone to think, Well, God doesn't have anything to do with this. But it says "whatsoever you do" — "do all in the name of the Lord Jesus." So it's pretty plain that if we want to follow Jesus, He wants to be included in everything. I have to work with this to keep my mind there.

This is Thursday morning and I want to get this on its "feet" again. There is a lot of activity going on in this house. As you

probably all know by now the Joe Coblentzes are living here with us
— the fourth week now. Yes, it sure is different with so many people.
There's nineteen children. Just had to think of that one woman
that is in my circle letter that remarried, and now they have twenty
altogether. But she is alone to manage the kitchen, etc. Guess I
depend much on Rachel. There are a couple of different possibilities
that they can maybe move to before too long. So we are waiting to see
what the Lord has, and in the meantime we are strengthening one
another.

Eli Millers, Rudy Millers, Harry (Butch) Yoder — (He's Rachel's
uncle). Then Emanuel Troyer and Emanuel Miller both bishops
from Ohio are here. We had baptismal services on Sunday....

This morning we are grinding some deer meat and wrapping it.
We have four here. Two are Joe's and two ours. Marion and Eli Ray
both have Deer B tags (same as doe tag) so that means they can get
two.

We had one snow that lay for a couple days, otherwise it is still
nice — for fall weather. This morning looks kinda cloudy. The men
have a couple days logging to do. They have time till November 30
yet. They have tried out the mules (in the woods) that we bought
over a month ago. They were hitched to the wagon but need some
more work yet. They are four- and five-year-old brothers — Jim and
Jack.

Well, is getting close to time to get ready. So must get going.
God's grace and blessings to you.

Ora Jay's

CHAPTER 15

The Choice

IRENE

Looking back, we can see that God had been working to plant seeds of truth in our hearts long before we moved to Montana. The first seeds were planted when we were in elementary school. Miss Bollinger, a non-Amish lady, would tell Bible stories with her felt board. She could make the stories so real that the characters really came alive. This was different — more exciting — than the simple stories that our parents read in the Bible storybook. Also, unlike the church sermons we heard, the stories were easy to understand.

The stories affected me at a young age, giving me the idea that I could pray to God and He would answer. One time in the fifth grade, I was nervous about a party I had to attend at school. I liked routine and didn't like wondering what a party would mean — what would I say? How would I act? What would we do? I became so nervous that I lost my breakfast. Still, I knew I had to go to school. I went to my closet and prayed — earnestly prayed for God to help me that day. This wasn't something I'd learned at home; we weren't taught that we could turn to God for help and strength. It was something I learned from Miss Bollinger's Bible stories.

And things were better that day in school. God took away my nervousness and showed me that He hears and answers prayer. Sometimes He answers in ways one would never expect. Now, years later, I was turning back to that same kind of faith.

"God, I feel so alone," I would pray time and time again. Through the months, as we encountered the disapproval of others in our community, we felt as though we were being torn away from all we knew. God took our security away from man. We were no longer secure in our church, our community, or with our friends and family. God was the only one we could turn to — and we turned to Him again and again.

In the West Kootenai, we were still sending our boys to the Amish school, where, each month, the school had a parent-teacher meeting. One time, Ora Jay was at work and had forgotten about the meeting. Instead, he and a non-Amish friend of his had planned for all of us to go on a picnic that evening.

"We can't go — the school meeting is tonight," I told him.

Ora Jay shrugged. "Oh, they could have it without us."

Anger, frustration, and worry built up within me. Tension filled my chest and tightened my gut. I could just imagine what people would say if we didn't show up. I just knew that we were already marked as being kind of rebellious, so if we didn't go, that would be the end of it.

I balled my fists and left the room. I was having a hard time.

"I'm not going to do it. I'm not going on that picnic," I mumbled to myself. "Ora Jay can go without me." Yet even though I was mad, I knew I couldn't do that. I had to listen to my husband.

We ended up going on the picnic, and two other families went with us. One of the other families even had children in the Amish school too, and since they weren't going to the meeting, I thought perhaps it wouldn't be that bad.

We found a beautiful spot for our picnic. All around me, nature reflected the Lord's glory — the meadows and the trees and the sky. Yet I set it in my mind that I wasn't going to enjoy myself. I ignored the songs of birds in the trees and brushed pine needles off my skirt. The boys ran around, playing with friends. Saretta clapped her small hands, watching them play and acting as if she wanted to join them.

Still, I had a hard time. Concern folded my eyebrows and my lips were pressed tightly. I just knew the next day I would have to face the teacher and the other parents. I knew that people were already wondering where we were. After we had finished eating, we gathered around the campfire to pray, as we always did when we gathered with our non-Amish Christian friends.

The others in our group knew I was having a difficult evening, and everybody prayed for me. As I sat there, hearing their words, I realized that I'd been running. So fearful was I of what would happen if we stopped being Amish that I'd been running away from God. He had brought so many wonderful people into our lives. He'd also spoken to us in His Word time and time again. He wanted to draw me to Him, but I kept looking back. Like Lot's wife, I was looking back at what I would be leaving behind. I knew I could never go forward — our family could never go forward — if I kept turning my attention to all I'd grown up with.

Come to Me. Follow Me. God's whisper wasn't audible, but it was a feeling deep in my soul. I'd seen a change in my husband. It wasn't an overnight change but a gradual drawing closer to God, allowing His Spirit to come in, and I wanted the same.

"I choose You, Lord." I didn't mouth the words, but the prayer came from deep within. It was then that I gave my heart to the Lord. I decided doing things my way — and even the way I was taught — wasn't worth it. Trying to cling to my Amish ways wasn't worth giving up a relationship with Christ.

I dared to glance up into Ora Jay's smiling face. He was looking at me, studying me. Could he see the peace in my eyes — the peace I felt deep in my heart? There was the same care and attention in Ora Jay's gaze that I'd seen yesterday, and the day before that, but now I understood it, understood him better. God had been working in his heart for much longer, and I'm thankful he'd been patient with me. We were on the same page now ... and it was a good place to be.

ORA JAY

In the months before that evening of the picnic, we had been associating with some non-Amish friends, praying and spending a lot of time together. The Lord had planned that for us because He knew we needed it, but this evening was the climax. We ended that evening with prayer, as we always did, but before we were done, Irene had given her heart to the Lord, and everyone knew it.

After God touched Irene in that way, everything began to change. We felt the freedom to leave the Amish lifestyle, though we knew how much our departure would hurt our friends and family. They would think that by leaving, we were opening the door to worldly destruction and hell. Our hearts ached knowing our family and friends would think that.

Our Amish preachers had always taught that people go out into the world so they can have a license to sin. We also heard that many who left wished to come back because they longed for the community and social life that they used to have. "Many who come back say they wished they would have stayed," we were told. This was to warn us that we should never think of leaving in the first place.

To the Amish, "licenses to sin" are things like driving a car and engaging in pleasurable activities, such as going to the theater, fairs, the circus, races, or concerts. Even things like bowling, skating rinks, ball games, and the rodeo are looked down upon. During *rumspringa* rebellious kids do such things.

We were told that following the world brings pride, when you choose to dress nice, fix your hair, do your nails, and wear makeup. Worldly dress involves fancy shoes, pants for ladies, and store-purchased pants, ties, or hats for men. Wristwatches, rings, necklaces, earrings, and tattoos are also considered worldly.

Items of technology are frowned upon: computers, music players, televisions, musical instruments. Amish men and women don't believe one should get electricity off the pole, because it puts our dependence on the world. They don't believe in having electric appliances, such as electric beaters, a toaster, mixer, coffee maker, or microwave. Lantern light is used instead of electric lights.

Amish homes are decorated simply too. There should be no colored walls, picture windows, fireplaces, or cathedral ceilings, and curtains need to be plain and hang a certain way. All outside siding should be white or gray, and homes should be rectangular and simply done.

The Amish don't take photos of people, and they don't allow their photos to be taken. This means there are no pictures that captured our growing-up years ... all we have is what we remember in our minds.

While hiring a driver for a ride is allowed, using horses is considered more righteous. To work by hand is also more righteous — this includes milking, corn husking, haying, plowing, planting, and hauling manure (which means scooping by hand too!).

The Amish are never to drive a car or fly in an airplane. They don't ski, whether downhill or in water. They shouldn't use boats with motors or any recreational vehicles such as motorized bikes. There should be no rubber tires on the equipment either — only steel wheels.

Tractors were only allowed for belt power and have to be kept stationary. And if you have a tractor used in this way, you have to switch the wheels to steel. There was no freedom to design your own style of buggy, and an Amish person should only use a push mower.

These rules had made sense to us our whole lives, but now they seemed like an unnecessary burden. Why should such things matter? Wasn't it more important to put our attention — our focus — on Jesus Christ?

"What does God really want from us?" we'd ask. "Are we going to leave what we have? Are we going to neglect the light that God has given us? Should we listen to what people are persuading us to do? Or should we follow God even though it means leaving behind all we used to live by?"

Letter to Family

March 11, 1994

Dear parents and bro and sisters,

Greetings in Jesus' holy name! "There is no fear in love; but perfect love casteth out fear: because fear hath torment. He that feareth is not made perfect in love. We love him, because he first loved us" (1 John 4:18 – 19 KJV). So when we have fears evidently we do not have perfect love. That can be a daily prayer. To commit completely to God and have faith in Him. It also says unbelief is sin — something I have to work on, on my part.

This is Friday morn and I want to get this out today. Sun is shining brightly again. Have been having springlike weather but still some snow and ice around. Horses are out in the field trying to get those few green sprouts which you can hardly see yet. Should actually not be on pasture but not have very much room otherwise....

Sounds like you are having something interesting in school, Ida Mae. Am sure you've had your ups and downs. One thing we can always "take it to the Lord in prayer." John (our school teacher) expressed the other evening that he had more of a trying time or challenge that year. The last day is April 12 and picnic 16th. So it's not very far away.

We want to honor our parents and we do appreciate the many things they have done for us. The Greek meaning for honor is value, to prize, dear, most precious. It also says that if we cannot leave father, mother, wife or children for His name's sake, we are not worthy of Him. Those are hard words for us but it comes from the Scriptures so what can we do but accept it.

Well, must close. Let's keep praying for each other.

Ora Jay's

CHAPTER 16

Silenced

ORA JAY

One of the best things that happened in the West Kootenai community was Lester Graber becoming one of our preachers. Lester was open to bringing the *Englisch* into our church. Like us, he also became friends with some of our *Englisch* neighbors and started attending *Englisch* prayer meetings. From his sermons it was easy to tell that God was getting hold of his heart. That helped us to stick around, so we hadn't completely broken off fellowship with the Amish church.

Yet when word got out that Lester and his wife, Rebecca, had started going to the non-Amish prayer meetings, many people started to talk. "How can this be? How can we have this … he's our preacher!"

Everything came to a head the weekend when Lester and Rebecca attended non-Amish family camp meetings at Dickey Lake on Friday and Saturday and then spoke at the Amish church on Sunday. Of course we loved everything he had to say. Finally someone was preaching the things that needed to be said. Because of his association with the *Englisch*, however — and his messages — church members wanted to silence him. To be "silenced" is a first step before "shunning." It allows the church member to remain in church, but they cannot speak in services or give their opinion. It takes away their authority. They wanted Lester to come to church but not to preach.

One evening, the week before the vote on whether or not to silence Lester and Rebecca, some of the men from the church came to our house to talk to us about our vote. You see, in the Amish church the whole church votes on whether or not someone should be silenced — and everyone must agree. The men were going around and talking to people ahead of time. They were doing it quietly, just to get everyone's opinion.

I told them that I couldn't vote. I would vote to support Lester, but I also felt that if this measure is what the church wanted I wasn't going to stop them. That Sunday, when the vote came before the church, Lester and Rebecca were asked to go stand outside while the church voted. Instead of voting, Irene and I went outside and waited with them.

That was a big moment for us. We had to ask ourselves, "Are we going to go along with this to make other church members happy? Are we going to be swayed?" We decided, "No, we are not going to be swayed."

As I stood there beside Lester a stirring happened within, and I lifted my gaze to the mountains surrounding the West Kootenai. For the last few months I'd been so focused on the issues of the church that I hadn't taken time to look up to God. God reminded me then that He created those mountains and had control of this situation too. In that moment I felt a sense of freedom. Later, the worries came back and burdened my heart because I knew Irene and I had a lot of decisions to make. Since we stood beside Lester, many of the Amish church members started excluding us, turning their backs on us as well. They could not get an unanimous vote the first time, as we had friends who knew our hearts. Still a dividing wall was coming up between us and our church, brick by brick.

One day, as I walked up the dirt road with an Amish friend who was also questioning his part in the church, I was pouring out my heart. It hurt to feel excluded, yet at the same time I felt God asking us to take steps of faith and walk away.

"Ora Jay, why don't we just go up in the woods here and pray?" he suggested. If anyone understood my pain he did.

We walked into the woods, shaded by tall pines and larch. Pinecones littered the ground. The air smelled of earthy loam, and the ground was damp. Layers of dead pine needles and aspen leaves covered the earth, making a soft carpet. Birds sang from the treetops. Rays of sun arched over the mountains and filtered through the branches, falling on our shoulders. We bowed our heads. The prayer strengthened me for that day, for that moment.

During that time I continued to have a real concern for the people in the Amish church. As I grew in my relationship with God I would think, "These people have got to see the truth." It's that thought that kept us going back to the Amish church instead of walking away and attending the community church, Kootenai Christian Fellowship. If the Amish church members wanted to shake us off, tough luck. I stuck like a burr. They couldn't shake us loose, and we kept returning. Maybe I was a thorn in the flesh to them, but I couldn't give up. Not yet.

Of course, there are two halves to every relationship, and the Amish church wanted to show us that they disapproved of the messages we had to share. A few weeks later there was another vote, and Lester and Rebecca were silenced. And then — Irene and I were silenced too. Even though our friends knew our hearts, they were later convinced — by more vocal church members — that there was disobedience to the church, so they felt justified to agree to silence us.

In May 1994 a knock came on the door, and I was surprised to see our landlord. "I'm sorry to say this, but I'm not going to be able to rent the house to you anymore. I need you to move right away."

"Right away?" I thought about our property and the house we had just started to build. We only had the basement in, and there was so much work to be done. "Can we wait a couple more months . . . so we can be closer to having our place ready?"

"No, I really need you out by next week."

"Next week? Do you have someone to live here?"

"Yes, and I need it by next week."

I knew what others were saying — that we were not living as an Amish couple should. They said we were making our choices for convenience's sake.

As we prepared to move into a home with no water and no electricity, it was clear that we weren't doing it for convenience.

"Do we have to move so quick?" Irene asked. "Can you talk to him again?"

"I called on our landlord and pleaded with him to give us more time," I told her. "He said someone else needed to move in right away. We have no choice, Irene. We have to move."

"We'll make do." Irene offered me a sad smile. Later, in the quiet of the night, I guessed the tears would come. The truth is, we both shed more tears leaving behind many of our Amish traditions than we did losing the girls. With our girls we were assured they were in heaven and better off than being here. But this — stepping away from some of our Amish traditions and stepping toward Christ — meant walking away from everything. It meant hurting our family. It meant displeasing our friends. To be an Amish person meant we knew how to dress, how to act, what to believe, and how to live. Now all of that was in question. How did we know what to do? How could we continue to stand strong when all we knew was stripped away from us — by our own choice?

I walked around with a heavy heart. As we packed up our things in the barn, the reality of what was happening hit us. We wept together and prayed. We also built closer friendships with others in the community who had left the Amish church.

As we continued our faith walk, we knew our choices didn't just affect us; they affected everyone around us too, including the Amish church members.

"Don't you remember the words in 1 Corinthians 9?" one Amish friend asked. "Jesus made himself a slave to everyone to win as many as possible. Why don't you just stay here — stay Amish — to win some?"

That made sense to me. It would also make things easier. We could keep our traditions, our faith, and our friends and share the good news with them ...

Yet as we continued to read, God's Word wasn't going to make things easy for us to straddle both worlds.

One day Irene and I were reading 2 Corinthians, and this verse stood out. It is one we had known our whole lives, but now we read it differently than before.

> For we are the temple of the living God; just as God said, "I will dwell in them and walk among them; and I will be their God, and they shall be my people. Therefore, come out from their midst and be separate," says the Lord. "And do not touch what is unclean; and I will welcome you." (6:16 – 17 NASB)

The words stopped us in our tracks, and we looked at each other.

Our whole lives we had worked to be a part of them — of the community. The goal was to not stand out, to humble ourselves, to think of others in the community above ourselves. We had learned this verse growing up. We had been taught that it meant to be separate from the world (anyone who wasn't Amish), but now it meant something different. Was God asking us to be separate from the traditions we knew so we could understand the fullness of His grace better? Was there freedom in serving Him?

At the same time our Amish friends were making their disapproval clear, the *Englisch* around us welcomed us and continued to ask us to join them in Bible discussions and prayer. During our time with these Christian families, we learned how to pray and how to think biblically. We had wonderful discussions about the Bible, and many of the burdens that I'd carried for so long began to lift. I learned that I did not have to be good enough to earn heaven. I learned that there were others outside the Amish community who loved God and served Him. We'd also been taught, being Amish, that it was "us against them," yet it was the "them" that was teaching me more about God and His Word than I'd ever known.

I changed on the inside too, and, looking back, I know that God was pouring out His Spirit on me. I never got together with the non-Amish when I didn't end up praying or coming away with a new thought or insight. More than once, as a new friend explained a Scripture verse, I'd say, "I didn't know that's what that Scripture meant." As I read, I came across new stuff I didn't even know was in the Bible. I realized then what a treasure God's Word is — something I'd always known but never fully grasped.

As Irene and I discussed that verse from Corinthians, we came across another verse: "And no one pours new wine into old wineskins. Otherwise, the wine will burst the skins, and both the wine and the wineskins will be ruined. No, they pour new wine into new wineskins" (Mark 2:22).

Inside, I felt like new wine. God had never felt closer. The more I turned to Jesus, the more I felt like a new person, and it seemed impossible to hold this newfound faith within our old Amish traditions. For example, it was common for the Amish to emphasize Matthew 7:13 – 17: "Enter through the narrow gate. For wide is the gate and broad is the road that leads to destruction, and many enter through it. But small is the gate and narrow the road that leads to life, and only a few find it."

When our preachers and parents talked about the broad road, they would tell us that it was the way of the world. The broad way was the easy way, the world's way, the convenient way. And the narrow road, we heard more than once, was "as narrow as one man's foot," so narrow that you could easily miss it. "Narrow is the gate to heaven," we were told, "and only a few are allowed in. There is hardly room for anyone."

While living the Amish lifestyle, I had wanted to be one of the ones who made it in, so I turned my attention to being more diligent about being a good Amish man and following the rules of the community. I compared myself to others, making sure I was just a little bit better than most. Then, somehow, hopefully, I would be good enough to get ahead of them.

But as I read more from God's Word, I realized the Bible was sometimes in conflict with our Amish rules. One day as I was working in the West Kootenai area, a fellow Amish man pulled out his GPS to show me how it worked. It was so modern — this new technology — but he could tuck it into his pocket and no one would say much about it. Yet if the man went and purchased an old 1940s beater truck it would be too worldly! There was a double standard, and some convenient things like GPS devices, electric mixers, and sewing machines (run with a generator) weren't given much thought because they could be tucked away and hidden.

Irene and I also started considering the words to the hymns we always sang in Amish services. Amish hymns are drawn from a collection called the *Ausbund,* which was first printed in 1564 and is the oldest Christian songbook still in continuous use. At the core of the *Ausbund* are fifty-one songs written by Anabaptists from Passau, Germany. These hymns embody the prayers of those jailed for their beliefs in the dungeon of Passau Castle from 1535 to 1540. The words of the hymns brought peace to us as we faced a different type of persecution, and we realized that in the Amish church we'd often sung the words without truly understanding the meaning.

> *The one who is not faithful in the smallest thing,*
> *and who still seeks his own good which his heart desires —*
> *how can he be trusted with a charge over heavenly things?*
> *Let us keep our eyes on love!*
>
> AUSBUND 119:14

Walking through this time with Irene reminded me of my school-days as a child. Just as the teacher used to explain the teachings in the textbooks, I felt as if God was teaching us now. I saw my non-Amish friends walking in Christ, growing in their relationships with Him, and praying together in unity. I would talk to family or friends from Indiana, and they'd discuss council meetings, dividing churches because of growth in the communities, and the need for another preacher. We were hovering between a world strictly ordered and dependable, and a walk with God that focused on grace and truth. You'd think steps toward grace would be easy to take, but they were made with uncertainty. After all, it was so different from how we'd been raised. What if our friends and family were right? What if we were being drawn away by our own ungodly motives?

In the end we found ourselves going back to God's Word. We weighed the things we'd grown up learning and discovered that many of them were manmade rules that hindered, not helped, a relationship with God. In an effort to live in humility and piety, those we loved most in the world were walking in bondage, and they didn't realize it. Of course, the Christian church outside of the Amish community sometimes does the same thing, depending on rules to help us make better choices. Why do we work so hard setting up idols and then try to appease them? Irene and I had to unlearn a lot of things so that we could learn them again God's way.

CHAPTER 17

A New Foundation

IRENE

We were forced to move into our new house when it wasn't much more than a foundation. We lived primitively in an unfinished basement for the first couple of weeks. It was a year before we had electricity.

We cooked over an open fire and hauled water for all our needs. I couldn't believe we were living this way — or that it had come to this. We were still a part of the Amish church, but we felt distant from everyone — family and friends alike.

My mind tried to wrap itself around all that would happen if we left the Amish for good. Ora Jay's suspicions were right about the rental house. Our being asked to leave had more to do with our decisions — and with being silenced — than anything else. No one moved into the rental right away. It sat empty even as we struggled to live in our basement home. In fact, that house sat empty for seventeen years!

When we considered leaving the Amish, we not only had ourselves to think about but our children too. I thought about their future spouses. I almost could not bear the thought of having "outsiders" for in-laws. We had always heard bad things about young girls not knowing how to run a household. Would a future daughter-in-law be able to cook, can, sew, and take care of children like a woman should?

For the first two weeks we had no water in the house. Instead, we put milk cans on the back of our buggy, and an Amish bachelor down the road let us fill our cans from his supply tank. For baths, the boys would grab a bucket of water from the heating kettle, and head back into the woods someplace to take a shower. They'd take some soap and then rinse off with a bucket of water. We also had an outhouse. The funniest thing is that we were pretty much shunned by the Amish church yet we were living more Plain than any of them!

In addition to cooking on a wood-burning stove, we had to heat the water for our laundry too. I had a large wash tub, and the boys would take turns lighting the fire to heat the water. At that point our boys ranged in age from teenagers all the way down to just starting school. Though some were still young, Ora Jay taught them how to be big helpers.

One day nine-year-old LeRoy and five-year-old Gerald stepped outside with me, ready to help light the fire for the laundry.

"I'll put water in the kettle if you light the wood," I told LeRoy. "Remember, don't use too much of the diesel. All you need is a splash to get the fire going," I warned him.

I headed back inside to sort through the laundry when a screech filled the air. At first I thought it was an animal. Then I realized it was Gerald's cry. I looked out to see his pants on fire! I ran out and helped him roll on the dirt to put it out.

His screams continued. The other boys raced to the house to see what happened. The smell of burning flesh filled the air. LeRoy picked Gerald up and stuck him into the water tank nearby.

Later, as I helped him ease onto the sofa, I saw that his leg looked blue, and I realized the fabric of his pants had melted into his leg.

We used a neighbor's phone to track down Ora Jay.

We cared for Gerald the best we could, soaking his leg in small bathtubs and giving him pain reliever. We called people around to come and pray for us, and it took many months for the wounds to heal. Weeks went by and seeing his pain was hard to take. Ora Jay had to carry him everywhere. It had been an accident, but Ora Jay and I knew what people were saying. They believed the accident occurred because we'd been disobedient to the Amish church. Still, we continued to make changes. We attempted to walk in God's freedom, but every attempt had us walking with quivering knees.

ORA JAY

Even after we moved to the basement house, another group of church members came. "You know what's going to happen to you if you keep going to the *Englisch* church and prayer meetings, don't you? Seeing that you're not coming back and that you're disobedient to the church, we're going to have to stop fellowshipping with you."

"And what have we done wrong? Can you turn to the Scriptures and tell us?" I'd ask.

"You're just too worldly."

I understood what they meant. We were disobedient to the church. We went to *Englisch* prayer meetings. We associated with the non-Amish and were friends with the *Englisch*.

One week an Amish preacher from Ohio came to town, and church services were to be held at Johnny Miller's. We decided to go since the Millers were friends of ours and we wanted to please them. When we walked into the Amish church, all eyes turned toward us but then quickly looked away. After the service, those we considered our friends occupied themselves with other people, other conversations. People didn't know what to say to us. We were walking in dangerous territory. Word gets around quickly when one is living as others believe they shouldn't.

Soon the Amish church leaders decided they simply couldn't do anything. So we were officially cut off, or shunned, by the church. We no longer had a voice in the congregation. We could not practice the handshake with a holy kiss as a greeting. To the Amish, the handshake and holy kiss are signs of unity, and in their eyes we were no longer unified.

Now our greeting was a handshake only. This was an obvious sign of a rejection for a rebellious person. Being silenced was a hard place to be. And those who were considered our friends were uncomfortable around us, yet they had to do their duty and reject us too.

Even though we were standing on what we knew was right and we knew that God was on our side, we did not see the whole picture of what God was doing. We understand now that if we weren't going to willfully, peacefully walk away from the Amish church, God was going to help us — by getting us pushed out.

IRENE

After the meeting at Johnny Miller's, I was surprised when the wife of one of the preachers approached me. "Can't you just come back and be like you used to be? You just need to be satisfied, Irene, with how things are and not search for other things. Things can be good here," she urged me.

My heartbeat quickened, and even though the words were simple, I sensed the emotion behind them. I looked at Ora Jay, and a knowing look passed between us. The awkwardness we felt made it easier to decide to leave for good, although our hearts were heavy.

After every church service the Amish have a fellowship meal together. This was usually one of my favorite times of the week, a chance to catch up with friends while the men chatted together and the children played. The meal was always simple — homemade bread, peanut butter spread, jam, pickles, and beets. Legs were added to our benches to turn them into tables, and the men ate first, followed by the women and children. I worked with the other women to lay out slices of bread. That day we had pie, and no one said a word to me as I sliced large pieces of apple pie and put them on paper plates.

The pie looked delicious, but I had no appetite. The tension in the room was too heavy. It seemed as if every woman's gaze was on me. I felt naked before them. Would it be too much to ask Ora Jay if we could leave early?

Still, the thought of leaving the Amish was unbearable. I knew how much rejection I would get, but that didn't stop me from hurting. And if the rejection of neighbors hurt this much, how would I ever face my family — those I loved deeply? My thoughts turned to my *dat* — who was a bishop. At one point, I thought I'd read a little more Scripture and see if I couldn't prove my husband wrong, but then of course I just ended up discovering more truth as I read.

One morning, when we were deciding whether to go to the Amish church or the church in town, I couldn't bear the thought of not going to the Amish church. Then Ora Jay showed me Galatians 3:28, "There is neither Jew nor Gentile, neither slave nor free, nor is there male and female, for you are all one in Christ Jesus." I thought, *Well, this is black and white, what can I say?*

Still, our whole lives, up until our move to Montana, we had always thought we would be Amish.

We continued to get letters from our family and friends in Indiana who knew our dissatisfaction. One letter from my dad suggested, "Why don't you move to Michigan where there are smaller Amish communities, so that you can be satisfied?" But we knew that what we sought couldn't be found in an Amish church.

In the spring of 1994 we decided not to attend the Amish church anymore and to start attending the Kootenai Christian Fellowship. We made this decision — like other family decisions — with our boys. They hadn't been ingrained with the Amish teachings as we had, and they were often able to give us a good perspective.

We talked to them about getting a phone, concerts we wanted to attend, and other possibilities. They pointed us back to God and what He wanted. "Does the Bible say there is anything wrong with that?" they'd ask.

During this time Eli and Marion both dedicated their lives to the Lord. This was a great confirmation to us that we were on the right track. One of our goals in coming to Montana was to build a good relationship with our boys, and now they had relationships with Christ! What more could we desire?

Around this time we went back to Indiana by train. Saretta was still an infant. This was our last visit there as Amish people. Even though we had changed, we still considered ourselves Amish. We'd tried to keep quiet about the changes for as long as possible because we knew that persecution would get worse when word got out. The hardest part is that we didn't have the right words to explain our changes to those steeped in tradition. So even as we visited — going from home to home — we made sure not to mention much about our life in Montana.

At that time the Indiana Amish didn't challenge us much, since we still dressed Amish and didn't drive a car. Seeing us like this didn't match with what they had heard about us. Meeting each new person, never knowing if they would challenge us, made us nervous. Not being able to talk about God and the Bible was in many was reassuring because it meant that God was taking us further into Himself. It was inspiring to know God's truth even when the world was against us.

The changes started small. After returning to Montana, I bought fabric that wasn't considered Plain. It had a small print, but I thought it would make a pretty dress. Later Ora Jay pointed out another fabric he thought I should buy — blue with darker blue roses. I wasn't sure. It was almost too showy, especially with those roses. It wasn't Plain at all. With a pounding heart I bought it.

I also stopped wearing my *kapp*. Instead I wore a small veil on my head. Many of the women in Kootenai Christian Fellowship wore them, so it was a doable step for me.

Ora Jay started making changes too, including a barber haircut. At first the haircut wasn't much different than an Amish cut, perhaps because it had been ingrained in our hearts that if we ever cut our hair we were being rebellious. That's what *rumspringa* boys did. That's what rebels did.

Ora Jay began wearing a hat with a bill instead of an Amish brimmed hat. He justified this by telling himself it was almost the same, just that the rim had been cut most of the way around. To get an Amish man to wear a bill hat to town, you might as well put a noose around his neck, because it would never happen.

We also got a telephone. The first time it rang we all jumped and felt as if we had just done the most horrible thing. My heartbeat quickened, and I wondered if this was what God wanted from us after all.

For Ora Jay and me, it was as if we'd had the same teacher all our lives and had been diligent students as we'd taken notes and followed all the rules, but then one day we got a new Teacher, and He was asking us to tear up our old notes and throw them away. He had a different way. We had to learn to get our thoughts and actions from the Tree of Life, rather than the Tree of the Knowledge of Good and Evil. And with each change we were being watched, being accused.

And things didn't get easier. I'll never forget the expressions on the faces of those in the Amish community after we got our first vehicle. They knew we'd lost our minds for sure ... and were going down the wrong path.

But while we were silenced by our Amish church, our fellowship with our *Englisch* friends continued. We joined with them for prayer meetings and now we had some of these meetings at our home.

I remember one funny event. We had a prayer meeting at our house while we were still living in the basement. Lester Graber went outside to do necessities (as we didn't have indoor plumbing). He had to go up a couple of steps to the top of the knoll. The boys had poured water on their sledding trail that went down the hill right close to the top of those steps, and Lester stepped on that icy spot and he went sliding down the hill to the bottom! He had no way to stop. He came back in laughing and told us the story!

Yes, there was laughter and joy even in the midst of the sorrow.

Letter to Family

May 12, 1994

Dear loved ones,

Greetings in Jesus' holy name! "Let us therefore come boldly to the throne of grace, that we may obtain mercy and find grace to help in time of need" (Hebrews 4:16 NKJV).

Wouldn't this be saying that we should boldly come before the Lord in prayer and by lifting up His name to overcome Satan (in time of need) when he tempts us?

This is Thursday morn. And sun is shining again beautifully. Early this morning we had a few sprinkles of rain. Hardly enough to settle the dust. Is very dry already and some places there's probably several inches of dusty powder.

We moved back here to our property this coming Saturday, two weeks ago. It wasn't really ready but it is livable and cheaper than paying rent. It's just good for the boys to be hauling water, heating water in an iron kettle to wash clothes (under the trees). We had promised the landlord a while back that we'd move. So with very short notice he asked that we should be out by May 1. At least it's spring to be living this way instead of fall. We are just in the basement with plastic on the main floor for a roof—no log walls yet. Although the logs lay here and most of 'em peeled. So we have many blessings that God has given us, even if we don't have all the luxuries.

We have a little boy laid up right now with a pretty badly burned leg. On Saturday LeRoy and Gerald were supposed to perk up the fire under the iron kettle. LeRoy poured some diesel fuel on the fire, and it poofed and spilled some diesel fuel on Gerald's pant leg. The fire started to creep out on the grass and Gerald started stomping on it and it caught on his fueled pant leg. Praise God there was a water tank close by and LeRoy dunked Gerald in there. There are some second- and third-degree burns. We didn't take him to the doctor but called him and got a prescription of "silvadine," which is very good medicated cream for burns. Also went to John Kathryn for some advice (they had an experience with John Kauffman's Kathy). So have been changing bandages two times a day and was encouraged last night how it seemed to be. He doesn't walk at all but is very patient with it all. So God has been very merciful in answering prayers.

Yes, we have our tickets for next week but guess we really have been wondering if we can go at all because of what happened to Gerald. The tickets were cheap but are nonrefundable so it's either go or lose the money. Guess the time and money seems almost impossible too but guess we'll see how the Lord provides. So you'll see us if we come.

We have most of the garden planted but nothing up except greenhouse things. Would like to get some plants somewhere yet. We planted around 500 strawberry plants and some raspberry plants. Both from other gardens. The big project yet is the irrigation we have to get in order. Last week the well driller was here, and we found water but we have no way to use it yet. No pump. Thank God we didn't have to dig too awful deep and it pumps twenty gallons in a minute — which is a good flow.

Yesterday Joe's Lois was here to help. She raked some dirt and made a pair of pants for Gerald. Not quite done though.

We want to wash today. Make a lot of dirty clothes with no grass, and Ora Jay also has been working in grease this week. He got a skidder (for logging big stuff) and now had problems before he got it home. He went to Canada today again about parts.

Well must get this to mailbox.

Remember us in prayers will do likewise.

Ora Jay's all

ELI RAY

Since my parents had a personal relationship with God, I saw what it was like to live for God. I wanted that same thing. So I tried with all my might to do everything right. It went okay sometimes, but other times I failed miserably. One summer afternoon in 1993, when I was thirteen, I lost my temper. I got really angry with my brother for something (I don't remember what). I knew I had blown it again. I could not get it right. I could not do it. I could not please God on my own.

In desperation I went into a half-built chicken shed and fell to my knees. There I gave up. I gave up myself, my life to God. I asked Him to forgive me. I asked Him to come in and take over my life. What a relief! What a peace! I felt like I could fly. I found that I did not have to perform; I just had to surrender my life to God.

For the next couple months I had sweet communion with God. I talked with Him every day. He and I went together everywhere. At that time I was still going to the Amish school. I remember praying to God, even in school.

After a while, I realized that I needed to share with someone what I had done and what had happened to me. I had read Romans 10:8 – 13: "But what does it say? 'The word is near you, in your mouth and in your heart' (that is, the word of faith which we preach): that if you confess with your mouth the Lord Jesus and believe in your heart that God has raised Him from the dead, you will be saved. For with the heart one believes unto righteousness, and with the mouth confession is made unto salvation. For the Scripture says, 'Whoever believes on Him will not be put to shame.' For there is no distinction between Jew and Greek, for the same Lord over all is rich to all who call upon Him. For 'whoever calls on the name of the Lord shall be saved'" (NKJV).

And Matthew 10:32 – 33, "Therefore whoever confesses Me before men, him I will also confess before My Father who is in heaven. But whoever denies Me before men, him I will also deny before My Father who is in heaven" (NKJV). I knew I had to confess Him before men.

What really motivated me finally to confess before men was my brother's conversion.

I remember one Wednesday night prayer meeting at our house. I showed interest because we had non-Amish company, and they were talking spiritual things in "our" house. With my new faith I had a great hunger for spiritual things. At this prayer meeting, they talked about my brother's conversion. They congratulated him and rejoiced with him. I knew I wanted that as well. To publicly identify with the others.

So I nervously stayed up when all my siblings went to bed and I told my parents all about my faith. What a great feeling to know that I was following God and what He said. Plus, my parents were glad. Perceptive as parents are, they had seen a change in me and had suspected a faith, but were only waiting for a confirmation.

After about two and a half years, when I was sixteen years old, I took the step of baptism. Another stepping stone in my walk of faith. After giving my testimony, I was baptized in Dickey Lake at the Bible Camp. I came up out of the water with a renewed desire and commitment. I felt like a new man, basking in God's grace. This is a place I always want to be.

CHAPTER 18

Our First Vehicle

ORA JAY

When we first moved to Montana, I worked for my uncle, building homes, but through the years I found myself working other various jobs. One type of work that I liked was logging. You may not believe this, but Amish men even do horse logging.

Montana mornings have a nip of chill on the air, even in the summer. We'd head out into the woods to log when there was still dew on the ground. It was a quiet place, and the silence was welcoming. Going out in the woods, in my opinion, is far better than working in a mill or factory in Indiana. It was even better than working on a farm.

The thing about logging is that it's dangerous. Since the Amish don't drive, and the areas we logged were far up in the mountains, we'd hire a driver to drop us off. But that meant we were out there on our own without transportation or a cell phone. More than once I told myself that if there were an emergency we'd be in big trouble.

Still, I liked logging because I could do it with my boys. Marion and Eli started working with me when they were about twelve and fourteen. This raised a few eyebrows, especially among the forest service people, who would often come by to check out what we were doing. "You know, you're not supposed to have boys in these woods, working like that. They need to be eighteen years old," one of the forest service rangers told me one day.

"Don't call them boys. They're men," I countered. "They do the work of men."

The ranger backed off and allowed it. Later, my sons told me that they'd overheard the conversation, and my calling them men had made a big impact on them. A father's respect is what every young man longs for, and they had mine.

For years we worked side by side, breathing in the fresh air and watching the wildlife. At lunch we'd stop, sit under a tree, and often take a short nap. I was proud to be able to tell my Amish friends, "The boys and I are together every day, working as a team."

This was the dream of every Amish man. That's why so many Amish men have farms, so that they can work alongside their sons and pass on their work ethic and skills to the next generation. As my sons became journeymen under me, we communicated and fellowshipped throughout the day. We knew each person's part in the task and what the other was thinking and doing.

Yet still in the back of my mind was the question, "What if something happens?" I don't know if I could bear it if something happened to one of my sons, especially since I knew the danger. Feeling the burden of responsibility, I'd head into those woods every day with a prayer and a hope that we'd be fine.

IRENE

One day, Ora Jay approached me about buying a vehicle. I knew it had been on his mind. I'd overheard him talking to others about pickup trucks. I knew he was worried about being in the woods with the boys with no way to get out or get help if something happened.

Our non-Amish friends supported us as we prayed through our decision. Anytime we wanted the freedom in our hearts to do something other than what our tradition had taught us, we knew we had to put our trust in God. God is greater and more loving than any man or any manmade rules. It's amazing how God can set you free! The more of His love we accepted, the freer we were to serve Him. A vehicle didn't seem off-limits anymore, and I could tell my husband's mind was working, trying to figure out how to make it happen.

His plan was to go down to Kalispell with a friend, get his license, and find a truck to buy — all in one day. Oh, yes, and his plan was to drive it home too, which made me nervous.

That day an Amish friend stopped by, and as we chatted about life, I thought, *You have no idea what my husband is doing right now … you wouldn't be here if you knew.*

We had been silenced by the Amish church. We were considered "on the outside." Yet some in the Amish community still felt we would come to our senses, repent, and return to the community. I knew all that would change if my husband drove home with a truck. To the Amish, a vehicle is the breaking-off point — the point of no return.

Dinner was ready, and I expected Ora Jay any minute. Surely he'd make it for dinner, wouldn't he? Then I heard it. The sound of a vehicle coming up the driveway.

A pickup truck pulled up and parked outside the house. I peered out the window. My heart quickened when Ora Jay climbed out of the driver's seat, keys in hand.

The boys rushed out first. The older ones knew what their *dat* had been up to, but the excitement of the younger boys overwhelmed everything. "Whose truck is that, *Dat*? How do you know how to drive it? Can I drive it too?"

I walked to the front door and out onto the porch. Instead of answering them, Ora Jay lifted his gaze and looked at me. I nodded my approval, and peace flooded his gaze. And amazingly, I had peace deep down too. Something I never would have expected. I was amazed at how calm I was — how well I accepted the fact that we now owned a vehicle, when not long before I couldn't bear the thought of having one. I also knew this was the dividing line. We were now cut off from the Amish. This meant no more association, no more family, no more involvement. It also meant no more decision making. Ora Jay and I had finally made a decision about whether or not to break off from Amish roots; we'd severed them with the rumbling of a truck's engine.

ORA JAY

When I first brought up the idea of getting a truck, I imagined Irene's disapproval. We had grown up believing that a vehicle is "of the world." The Amish believe it breaks your connection with your community. Instead of staying within the area where you live — and connecting and caring for neighbors — a vehicle places you in the world of the *Englischers*, speeding up your life, and giving you no time for family or God.

I'd asked a friend to give me a few driving lessons, and then I headed down to the Department of Motor Vehicles. Still, it wasn't an easy decision. On the way to the DMV I kept telling myself I'd made the right decision, and it was a wise one. Yet the burdens from my youth were firmly planted on my shoulders.

For the Amish, having a vehicle is an unpardonable sin. If you died in a vehicle accident, you would most certainly not go to heaven. On the drive home, I had to ignore my thoughts: *What if I have an accident on the way home? Where would I be then? Where would my soul be?* Instead, I prayed, and the Lord gave me grace to trust in Him. My salvation is based on what He has done for me — and no vehicle could change that.

Still, for many months I was tense every time I drove that truck. First, because switching from horse and buggy to a motor vehicle is hard for an Amish man. He is used to gazing around when he's on the road, and he doesn't have to keep his mind on what is immediately ahead. He doesn't even have to stay awake a lot of the time. But you have to adjust when you drive a vehicle. You have to keep your eyes on the road and concentrate.

There were times when I didn't pay attention and a tire would go off the road. I'd quickly adjust. Once when I was heading up to a logging job with Marion and Eli Ray, I was messing with a portable tape player while going through an S-curve. Both wheels went off the road, and in a second the truck was flipped on its side.

I jumped from the truck in a rage, worried that Amish friends would see us. I imagined their smirks. Shame and worry carried heat up my neck.

I directed the boys to run to the closest house and call a friend for help. As I stood there, emotion building up in my chest, I heard God's still, quiet voice. *What are you so afraid of man for?*

I knew He was right. I was so concerned about being "found out" that I hadn't even taken time to thank God for keeping us safe.

A while later the boys arrived with Allen, an *Englisch* friend, who brought his pickup, and we were able to upright our truck and go on to work. I'd learned my lesson to keep my eyes focused on the road — and on God.

Of course, we never wrote any of these things in our letters. We never told our family that we attended an *Englisch* church or that we now wore *Englisch* clothes or that we had bought a vehicle. We knew these things would get back to them — news like this always found its way home. We also knew that when our family heard about our latest decision, we'd get a letter saying, "So, I hear you've bought a vehicle."

We knew of their disapproval, so we kept quiet about the changes. Instead, we added Scripture to our letters. We shared what was going on in our hearts with the hopes that they'd start to understand why we were making the decisions we were.

It was easier to open up to my family than to Irene's. My parents even came to visit us in Montana after they had returned from Mexico for medical treatments. We knew they disapproved of many things — and that more than anything they wanted us to remain Amish — but since both of them were facing health problems, they put their focus on just enjoying our family, which we appreciated. But for most people, the news of our decisions put a wedge between us — a wedge large enough to divide families — and the awareness of it broke our hearts.

Letter to Family

September 8, 1994

Dear loved ones,

First a greeting in Jesus, our Lord and Savior's name. "Let us draw near with a true heart in full assurance of faith, having our hearts sprinkled from an evil conscience, and our bodies washed with pure water. Let us hold fast the profession of our faith without wavering; (for he is faithful that promised)" (Hebrews 10:22 – 23 KJV). He says we should come closer to Jesus being assured that He has saved us if we accept it as a gift, but in faith. And let's hold to that faith we have in the Lord Jesus without doubting because He does what He promises. And of course as you know in chapter 11, Paul was relating a lot of incidents before Jesus' time that were done by faith (by believing). We can nowhere find that faith would mean a certain denomination — only faith in Jesus our Savior.

This is Thursday eve. And are waiting till the men come home for supper. We are having mashed potatoes, fresh beans, and hamburger gravy. First time we're having mashed potatoes with new ones, but was hungry for some so decided to make some. The beans is the last of them now. We had a light frost once that knocked 'em down a little. We had four quarts to can so filled three cans of potatoes to fill cooker. Our sweet corn did not do very well although we had several meals, but it was very spotty due to lack of nutrition in the soil. But God has been very good to us. He gave us sunshine and provided water for irrigation even if it did not rain much.

You probably heard that they are having forest fires here in the west. It was pretty close. Down near Libby they had some. But is slowing down some. They had hundreds of people in fire camps that helped fight the fires. And they get paid pretty good wages. Guess you have to wonder where all the money comes from. Heard say this was the worst fire, or rather the most fires since 1910. It was extra dry and hot this year but has rained some lately but can't see its evidence anymore.

Yes, we got a letter from Ida Mae today saying some things about the wedding. . . . We certainly wish them God's blessing in their married life together. We surely would not wish them trials or sorrows but without doubt that will come sooner or later. But that helps us to draw closer to God and put our trust in Him so it all has a purpose. . . .

Sorry we had these so long, come during a busy canning time. Hope everyone is well, thank God we are all healthy. Let's pray for each other.

Ora Jay, Irene, and all

Circle Letter, Grieving Parents Group

September 28, 1994

Dear friends,

First a greeting in Jesus' name! "Beloved, I pray that you may prosper in all things and be in health, just as your soul prospers" (3 John 1:2 NKJV). That is our prayer for you all. It really doesn't matter so much if you are prospering financially or not but just so your soul is prospering. Drawing closer to God and reading and learning more of His Word and ways. And to "exhort one another daily, while it is called 'Today,' lest any of you be hardened through the deceitfulness of sin" (Hebrews 3:13 NKJV).

This is Wednesday morning and I got bread dough started. Otherwise didn't get much accomplished. Just now some guys from the telephone company came to put in a telephone line. Seems with logging for our occupation, it is hard to do without. There's so many calls to make and so many want to return calls so it is very inconvenient at a pay phone or even a neighbor's. Praise the Lord that He put intelligence into man to invent it.

No, we still have not built on top of our basement. All summer it seems as if we will start just anytime now but it never happens. But we would still like to this fall if possible, but want to be patient with whatever the Lord provides. You may have heard that we are really having forest fires out here this summer. It is extremely dry — hasn't rained much at all since June. Just Sunday a fire started again that was on this side of our reservoir — about twelve to fifteen miles away from here. It was pretty breezy and traveled over hundreds of acres in a couple days. Have not heard much about it yesterday and today. We think it so bad all that wood is burned but there have been some blessing from these fires, we thank God for them. Sorry to have missed the gathering. Sounds like about everybody was there. Also sorry to have missed Harleys when they were here. Sheet's full. Let's pray for each other.

Ora Jay's all

Letter to Family

October 27, 1994

Dear parents,

    This is Thursday p.m. Time for scholars to come home any minute. The sun has been peeking through the clouds for about a half an hr or so. Had been drizzling all forenoon. Started yesterday p.m. already. Had my wash out then but was same as dry so got it in just in time. Had to take dampness out yet in here. I'm still washing outside but is getting to be chilly. In p.m. it's not too bad. We're planning to bring wash machine right in the house as there's one spot not jammed yet. We might enclose the front porch with plastic so that it might work there too. The drying part will be worse than the washing. Imagine having wash lines right through the crowded living quarters....

    Our boys go to school at Allen's. We helped put up the school-house this fall, which made us pretty busy. There are only thirteen scholars. Ramona Miller is their teacher. "Grace be with all those who love our Lord Jesus Christ in sincerity. Amen."

Ora Jay's all

Letter to Family

January 19, 1995

Dear parents and brother,

Grace be with you. Greetings in Jesus' name. Want to write a letter your way after supper. 7:30 Eli and Marion went to Ivan Bontrager's to practice for singing. They want to sing in church as a group. Kyle and Marion and two of Ivan's girls. Kyle is seventeen and was baptized this fall — has a heart for the Lord. LeRoy is washing dishes. Danny diddling with sewing machine. Had a very nice day again, sunshine all day. How does this find you? Hope all is well and healthy.

We need to trust the Lord with all our heart, mind, and soul. There is a lot of self-sacrifice to lay down ourselves that we trust in so much. We want to secure ourselves with something we feel secure like a system that appears to work. We fail to look into it for fear of our security that we have. When indeed if we secure ourselves in that we will go to hell. God wants to be the security of man's soul. It takes faith to follow God day by day. But does it really take faith to follow a system that keeps the law and uses manmade rules to keep it?

If we ask ourselves what would we do if we weren't put under a law? Is it robbing God's glory and not living by faith? "Whatever is not from faith is sin" (Romans 14:23 NKJV). Peter through faith walked on water till he looked to himself. We might say we can do better than Peter.

God requires us to believe Him and His Word and have faith to remove a mountain from our life. Do we have faith that He will show us and fill us, our soul, if we cry out to Him, believing? Do we think He can and will open our eyes to His Spirit and Word? Only if we have faith, not when our faith is in church or man.

I'm only writing from my experience of trying by myself to do His will. Always falling short and not having victory over my sins. The harder I tried, the stronger the temptation comes. I'm here to say there's only one way, that is falling on our face, crying out to God. The story in Romans talks about faith and the law. Paul was telling them how they think it's by the law they will be saved. But rather it's by coming to the light from being dead, living in faith. Read through chap. 8 and Galatians chap. 3. Of course there are more Scripture that verify the same.

This is again morn. I was reading in Matthew 15 – 16 this morning. When the scribes and Pharisees asked Jesus why the disciples don't wash their hands (ceremonially) before eating. They saw they didn't wash as they were used to and how their forefathers had laid out a tradition for them. So they challenged Jesus with that. So we can see how Jesus answered them. He accused them of violating the commandments of God by their traditions. He said they draw near to Me with their mouth but their hearts are far from Me. He enforced again that in vain they worship Me, teaching as doctrines the commandments of men. That what comes out of a man is what defiles him. He said every plan or tradition that is not planted by my Heavenly Father will be uprooted. And that blind were leading blind and they would both fall....

What do we have? Just a very good place to challenge us, where do we and how do we stand, do we see our need and cry to God for help? He is there to help in need, wanting to come in our heart fully surrendered to Him.

He puts it as a voluntary thing. If anyone desires to come after Me? To deny himself, take up his cross and follow Me. How is this possible? In the next verse He says whoever desires to save his life will lose it. But whoever loses his life for My sake shall find it. Is He talking about bodily death to be killed or when we stand for Christ regardless of people? To pick up His cross means to follow His will regardless and to deny all that we have and let God build us as His temple. He says for what profit is there to gain the whole world or all people and to lose our soul. Then He finished with "If we have this work, doing His will and picking up the cross, we will get His Father's reward." We have to understand that words outside of Faith and eternal life in God is of no avail.

Well, Marion's out cutting eight-foot logs to take to the mill. We can take about 125 pieces at one time. Which is around $600 (but with some expenses). I need to go help.

We are looking forward to our addition to our family. The Lord has blessed us with health in this. Pray for us as we need God's hand at all times. We will have the baby at a home in Kalispell at a friend's house. Lord willing. We would appreciate a visit from our parents at all times. We know it would be difficult on your part but what would Jesus do.

Your son and family

CHAPTER 19

Trials and Cares

IRENE

January 30, 1995, Steven Jay was born at Timothy and Elizabeth Heaps's house in Kalispell, with Elizabeth as our midwife. We decided to have the baby there because Elizabeth didn't have a driver's license at the time, and also because we were still living in the basement and did not have the conveniences we needed. Later, in the crowded basement, with the boys running around and filling the basement with noise, I rocked my baby, singing an Amish lullaby that I'd sung to all of my children.

> *Müde bin ich, geh' zu Ruh,*
> *Schliesse meine Augen zu;*
> *Vater lass die Augen dein,*
> *Über meine Bette sein.*
>
> *Ja, Jesus liebt mich,*
> *Ja, Jesus liebt mich,*
> *Ja, Jesus liebt mich;*
> *Die Bibel sagt mir so.*
>
> *Tired am I, go now to rest,*
> *And close my eyes;*

Father, let Thine Eyes
Watch over my bed.

Yes, Jesus loves me,
Yes, Jesus loves me,
Yes, Jesus loves me,
The Bible tells me so.

By this time, Gerald's burns had mostly healed. Then another horrible accident happened. Steven — at eight months old — severely burned his arm when he pulled a pot of hot tea onto his highchair tray from the table.

Also, just when Gerald was able to get around good again, he fell off the buggy and a wheel went over him and hurt his collarbone. Another time he got his heel in the bike wheel and hurt it bad enough to require stitches.

We again received the knowing looks from those we knew. They believed God was trying to get our attention, and He wanted us to return to the Amish. We saw these mishaps, however, as pokes from the enemy, trying to discourage us.

Circle Letter, Grieving Parents Group

March 8, 1995

Dear friends,

"Therefore, having been justified by faith, we have peace with God through our Lord Jesus Christ, through whom also we have access by faith into this grace in which we stand, and rejoice in hope of the glory of God" (Romans 5:1 – 2 NKJV). It says we have access to grace but only by faith and we can rejoice in the hope we have in God. How wonderful are God's promises!

I want to get this one on its road again. Sorry it had quite a stay here. I guess we find out that babies take time especially if they are somewhat fussy. Yes, we are blessed again through God with a baby boy. Steven Jay, weight eight and a half pounds, born on January 30, now five weeks old. Makes boy No. 7. Leaves Saretta kind of alone, but God knew what we needed so we will glorify Him....

May we all have Jesus as our Savior and guide.

So long,

Ora Jay, Irene, and all

Circle Letter, Grieving Parents Group

October 9, 1995

Dear friends,

Greetings in Jesus' most precious name! "This is the stone which was rejected by you builders, which has become the chief cornerstone. Nor is there salvation in any other, for there is no other name under heaven given among men by which we must be saved" (Acts 4:11 – 12 NKJV).

Yes, Jesus must be the cornerstone. When Peter and John healed the lame man at the temple, people started accusing them, even arrested them, asking them by what power or name they had done this. Then Peter was filled with the Holy Spirit and said ... Let it be known to you ... that by the name of Jesus Christ ... this man stands before you and there's no other salvation in any other name by which we can be saved. After that they even forbid Peter and John to speak or teach in the name of Jesus, but Peter and John would not listen to that and so much more prayed for boldness. In verse 31 it says, "They spoke the word of God with boldness." That can apply so well in our day, that people want to attach another name to their salvation and hardly acknowledge that Jesus Christ is our Savior. So that is my desire to speak the Word of God with boldness.

Wonder how this would find each of you in your homes? I guess I can't say that I can imagine you all in your homes as there's even two of you that we have never met, No. 5 and No. 8. We hope, though, that everyone is well and happy. We are all healthy and praising the Lord for His goodness to us.

We had another "burn" experience just last week. Saturday a week ago we were just preparing to eat (Ora Jay and two oldest were gone), and we had made a pot of tea and set it too close to the edge of table. While we were praying little Steve, eight months old, who was on a highchair, reached out and pulled the teapot off the table onto his tray and of course dumped out over him. Over his arm and leg. But praise God how fast it has healed already. The leg wasn't quite so bad and the bandages are almost ready to be left off. But the arm is worse and will take more time. Am sure doctor would probably suggest doing skin grafting but they had said that for Gerald too. It's not one and a half years that he had his burns on his leg and it's all healed nicely and says it's not more tender than the other leg. It of course has a scar but can't believe that grafting wouldn't leave a scar also. We have confidence in the Lord that He will heal it, so will take "one day at a time."

Are you about ready for winter? Doesn't seem like we are but am sure we'd take it if it came tomorrow. We have some potatoes to dig yet. The plants had been so green up till our killing frost which was over two weeks ago. They yielded very well again. We had a well moistured summer. Seems the root plants always do well out here. Like carrot and potatoes. The Lord provides so abundantly, and we praise Him for it. Ora Jay's folks are planning to come out to visit us in about a week and a half so we are looking forward to it. We wish God's blessing on you all.

So long,
Ora Jay, Irene, and all

ORA JAY

It took us longer to build our log home than we had expected. When we first moved in, we hauled sawdust to put on the wood of the main floor as insulation with tarps on top. We tried to slant it a little — enough to let the water run off. The first summer it was pretty good with no leaks. But with winter and snow and the settling of the sawdust by spring, we had many leaks that ruined some books and furniture, which was pretty discouraging.

Knowing it wouldn't last another winter, we worked hard to get the log walls up and ready to put the roof on before another winter. The church people of Kootenai Christian Fellowship helped us to get our roof on the new log house. We had a "frolic" one day in November '95. By the end of the day we had an empty shell with the roof on.

We appreciated the help and concern of the brotherhood. They not only helped us in a time of need, they also strengthened our faith.

In 1995 we had bought a timber sale, which looked like a good deal at the time. For a timber sale, one makes a bid to log a certain parcel. The bid is the price you pay for the wood. It's up to the buyer to make money — the profit is made between what you buy it for and sell it for. Then, the winning party has a certain amount of time to log the property and sell the lumber before the money is due to the government. Once you are the winning bidder there is no way to get out of it. The money is due when the money is due.

We were excited about winning the bid and had plans to log the land, when suddenly, the market went down. Any way we looked at it, we would not make enough money on the timber to pay the bid, so I chose not to log the land because I'd lose money.

Months passed, and we held off doing anything, thinking an option would turn up. The termination date was coming closer, and the deal was big enough that we faced potential bankruptcy. Irene and I were burdened by this, and the burden was great. The date clicked closer, and we were about to lose everything.

We called a meeting to pray about this. Just before our friends left, one brother so confidently said, "The Lord is going to answer this prayer. I don't know how, but I know He will." I remember thinking, *How can he say that so confidently?*

Then, one Sunday afternoon, as we were driving home from church, we saw that there was a forest fire. It looked like it was in the direction of our timber sale. Sure enough, that fire — which had been started by a lightning strike — had traveled three miles. It had burned into our timber sale far enough that they called it "catastrophic intervention." And that meant we were completely freed from the sale and didn't have to do a thing with it. Praise the Lord! We were so awed by how God answered that prayer. It was in a way we never would have thought of, and it was a faith builder! The due date for the money was only five days away, and now we were released. It showed us that we don't need to walk in arrogance about anything in our life. This very moment the sun — and every lightning strike — is controlled by God.

Sometimes I wonder, *Who am I that God would choose to love me and to mold me into Christ's image?* Yet God chose me, and He put a spirit within me that would yearn for Him. Everything happens because God is in control. What a great time that was to learn that I have absolutely no control. I'm at the mercy of God. It's wonderful to know my relationship is absolute. It's the best of the best, because God says so.

In the fall of 1996 we worked hard to finish the upstairs of the house — so it would be more than just a shell of the walls and roof

— so the boys could move up. In the spring of 1997 we finished the main floor and finally had elbow room!

Although we'd left the Amish church, most of the people there continued to treat us with kindness. Still, they worried about what others would think if they were seen with us. For example, if I saw an Amish man walking and offered him a ride, he'd quickly refuse. "If it were up to me, I wouldn't have a problem with it," he'd say. "But I better not do it to keep the peace."

Circle Letter, Grieving Parents Group

February 12, 1996

Dear friends,

Greetings in Jesus' name, name above all names. Who is our Savior, counselor, Prince of Peace and lots, lots more. "As you therefore have received Christ Jesus the Lord, so walk in Him, rooted and built up in Him and established in the faith, as you have been taught, abounding in it with thanksgiving" (Colossians 2:6 – 7 NKJV). To be rooted and built up in Him would be nothing else but getting familiar and having knowledge of the Scriptures and to have faith in God that His word is true and alive. Then in verse 8 it warns us though, "Beware lest anyone cheat you through philosophy and empty deceit, according to the tradition of men, according to the basic principles of the world, and not according to Christ." Which could be so many different things — carnal things that men have figured out and have knowledge of but if it's not Christ it's to no avail. Here is a phrase that I read yesterday. Which is a good explanation of faith. "The beginning of anxiety is the end of faith and the beginning of true faith is the end of anxiety."…

Sounds like more of you are enjoying grandchildren or at least in-laws. I guess we'll go on enjoying our babies. Ours is now over a year old. He's walking, teething, and chattering but not very many real words. Amazing what a short time they are a tiny baby. They make such a big change in their first year. I often think of that verse in 1 Peter 2:2 where it says, "as newborn babes, desire the pure milk of the word, that you may grow thereby" (NKJV). We know how much they desire to nurse especially when they are a little older. Do we too desire to read the Bible that much or are we that hungry for the Word so that we can grow all the time? Just a challenge for me.

Time to stop. Would like to write more letters.

May God richly bless you with His Word.

Ora Jay, Irene, and all

CHAPTER 20

A New Type of Dress

IRENE

I remember how hard it was attending the Kootenai Christian Fellowship at first. I couldn't believe how some people — women — were dressed. How could the preacher's wife look so nice? The women had ruffles and lace on their dresses! Most of them made their own dresses, but they made them so fancy and with prints. I had a hard time with that. What were the rules?

Every time we faced a new decision, I tried to figure out where the line was. Are musical instruments okay? Should women go without a head covering? What about appliances in the home? And surely women should *not* wear pants.

One time I talked with our friend Dick Harding about how confusing everything was. "I'm just not sure about who's supposed to be doing what. Who are *we* supposed to shun?"

He shook his head and smiled. "You don't have to worry about shunning anyone, Irene. Just show love. Love is what you're supposed to do."

That was a big challenge for me. It was hard to love people and not think, *This is right* or *That is wrong*.

There are many unspoken rules among the Amish. One is that a woman makes all the clothes for her family. Growing up, I sewed my own clothes. After I had my family, I sewed their clothes too. When someone wears *Englisch* clothes, it is clear that they are walking in the world. To the Amish, you are able to see from a distance if someone is a Christian by their dress. You could tell what was in a mother's heart by how she dressed her children. Some young Amish women put little fancy things on their babies, and everyone else would look at that and shake their heads. And it was a known fact that you would go to hell if you died wearing *Englisch* clothes.

"Don't get caught in the world," parents often told their *rumspringa* teens.

Once, after I stopped wearing my conservative Amish dress, I asked one of my sisters if she thought it was her Amish clothes that guaranteed her place in heaven.

"It won't save us and get us to heaven," she commented with a tilt of her chin, "but worldly clothes can keep you out."

The Amish in the community watched me closely as I went from wearing a *kapp*, to a veil or fabric head covering, to no head covering at all.

It got back to me what people were saying. "See, they're looking farther away. It just gets worse and worse."

They knew I was gone for certain when I wore jeans and cut my hair, but I discovered that the deeper I got into a relationship with Jesus Christ, the more freedom I had.

Ora Jay and I soon discovered that it was actually easier to share the good news of Jesus when I stopped wearing a head covering altogether. When I had worn a head covering, people would see me as somehow different. Their attention would be turned to my head covering, and they seemed to be thinking, *If that's what you have to share, I don't want it.* It divided people from us, as if it was still "us" and "them." Now I'm walking in the freedom from pins, hems, and head coverings. It's not in my vocabulary anymore.

My Amish family claims, "You totally lost it." But I say, "God has given us so much freedom in Him to look at Him and not at things." Love is so much easier than judging. It feels better deep inside too.

The more you focus on side issues, the less you focus on Christ, and you're wasting your time. The more you judge, the less you love. The more you love, the less you judge.

ORA JAY

One day while driving to Kalispell, I ran out of fuel. I hoped someone would stop and help, and someone did — a guy with long hair. He was kind and helped me, and then he started talking about God. I couldn't believe it. My whole life I thought I knew how Christian men were supposed to dress, supposed to look.

I went down the road another ten miles, and I ran out of gas again. Another guy stopped to help — another guy with long hair! And again we ended up talking about God.

After that God whispered to my heart about the judgments I made as soon as I saw someone. He reminded me not to judge people by their appearance.

If your religion teaches you to judge, then you will in turn be judged by others, and I realized I didn't want that.

The farther we walked away from the Amish tradition, the more freedom we felt to hear whispers of grace from God and to know that He was in control. We discovered Christ is all in all. There is nothing made that Christ isn't in.

We used to think of some things as evil, but they were really just "things": a tree, a rock, a radio, a horse, a television. We have the freedom to know that what's in the heart is what corrupts us — and even when we make mistakes, the blood of Jesus washes us good as new. We are not our own. We are His. Our dependence is on Him and not on ourselves. It's freeing not to have to look to man to decide what's wrong and what's right — things like the width of a hat brim or the pattern on a dress.

What's in our heart is what comes out of us. Love, trust, and all the attributes of the Holy Spirit. Instead of judging others, the closer we get to Jesus, the more we will esteem others more highly than ourselves. Those are the attributes God thinks about — not about how we use earthly things in certain ways.

Jesus Christ and His blood have set us free to be able to stand before God, knowing we are totally and absolutely clean — that our hearts are right. He is the One who created us. We are the clay that our Potter is forming. Our minds are being changed to God's way of thinking, which is so contrary to religious thinking.

As Irene and I continued on this journey, we felt like new people. We realized that even though we had been baptized into the Amish church, we'd done that according to tradition and not because of our relationship with Jesus. So we decided to get baptized again at Kootenai Christian Fellowship. Yet as soon as our Amish family found out about it, the news spread like wildfire. "How dare you have more than one baptism?" they'd say.

Yet it was easy to hold to these beliefs when we were far away from Indiana. It was even fairly easy when my parents came to see us. They did their best to not focus on the many changes. But the true test came when we returned to Indiana, to the people who knew that we'd been baptized in a different way, were driving a car, and were wearing *Englisch* clothes.

CHAPTER 21

How Can We Explain?

IRENE

In 1997, three years after we left the Amish church in Kootenai and two and a half years since we'd last seen my family, we traveled back to Indiana. Our vehicle wasn't working, so our friend Allen Miller let us borrow his Suburban. We were amazed by his generosity — giving without expecting anything in return.

Our stomachs were in knots the whole drive. We wanted to extend our love, but we knew that our lifestyle would be rejected.

We drove to my parents' place first. Even parking our vehicle in front of their house seemed wrong. My *dat* was a bishop, and I'm sure he worried about what the neighbors would think. Before we let everyone out of the car, I went inside to see if we could all come in. I remember what I was wearing — a lime-green dress with a small print. I wore a veiling as a head covering, but not a *kapp*.

My sister Ida Mae came to the door. As she looked at me her eyes grew wide. She gasped and a hand covered her mouth. "How can this be? Oh, Irene ..."

Tears filled my eyes yet I forced a smile. "May we come in?"

"Ja." She nodded, but the tension was clear.

Tears filled my father's eyes as we entered. I'd never seen him with tears in his eyes before. We didn't stay long, but they seemed to enjoy seeing the children. As we left, my father admonished us, "How can you do this?"

Inside, I asked myself a different question — after our transformation in Christ, how could we not?

Ora Jay's *dat* was more welcoming; "Hey, you guys!" he called out as the kids climbed out of the vehicle. Of course, Ora Jay's parents had seen us in our *Englisch* dress when they'd visited Montana. They'd eaten with us and rode in our cars, and we showed them Glacier National Park. The hardest thing was that when they returned home, they had to confess their misdeeds before the church, since we were under the ban.

Ora Jay and I hurried toward them and offered them hugs — the first hugs we'd ever given his parents. After that first day we sensed they were waiting to get a hug whenever we came or whenever they left. They'd never do that amongst themselves, but they appreciated them.

ORA JAY

Being in Indiana was hard. With such a tight-knit family, we knew they wanted us to stay Amish, not just for our sake, but for theirs as well — for their reputation. Irene's dad would say, "You're the only daughter who's done anything wrong ... I didn't think this would ever happen to me." They'd put a guilt trip on her, and it would just crush her. That was the hard part, along with the letters, the rejections.

Our first day back in Indiana, we walked into a relative's house, and everyone stopped talking and just stared at us. It was the first time they saw us in non-Amish dress. More than that, they had a look that said, "Whoa, they're here."

When someone is shunned, a separation is supposed to take place. You're not able to exchange money, like in business deals. Also, you don't sit down at the same time and at the same table as a shunned person, because the Scriptures say, "Don't sit and eat with a sinner." To get around that rule, my family would plan it so everyone could eat without a separation. They would set up the food cafeteria style, then everyone could go and fix their plate and sit down.

When we first came home for a visit, Irene's family would set a separate table for us, and that didn't feel good at all, though in recent years they have us eat cafeteria style a lot more. And they have come to accept us more than they did.

Irene's family also came to visit us in Montana. They would ride in the same vehicle, but they wanted our boys to drive, because our sons were never members of the Amish church. That's how it works. If you were never a member, you are better accepted and can do those things. We were there and could have done the driving — we would have loved to do it — but they said no. Over the years we have gotten used to these awkward situations and painful feelings. As Christ was persecuted, we were persecuted too. That gives us comfort. Also, when our families shunned us, they were actually hurting themselves more than they were hurting us.

For a while it was tempting not to go to their homes. We'd think, *They're not going to accept us anyway.* But we keep going and keep loving them as Jesus would. Today Irene's family struggles to accept us, but we still have good times together.

The most serious questions and reprimands come in letters, of course. As hard as it is, we do our best to answer them ... and to pray that our answers penetrate their hearts.

Letter to One of Irene's Sisters, Written in 1996

I want to try to explain (with the Lord's help) why we see some things so different than we used to. And I want to use the biblical way, as we know God's Words are true and that we can rely on no other teachings more than the Bible. "I am the way and the truth and the life. No one comes to the Father except through me" (John 14:6). Just Jesus and Jesus alone.

I would rather not even write this letter as it's going to be a hard one to write, but I am getting a burden more and more to write it. Not because I really want to try and tell you something. But because if we don't answer it will appear that we are just ignoring your concerns and letters or else you think we are hit so hard and we don't want to admit it. Guess I hardly know where to begin. It is sometimes so hard to accept the fact that we are not accepted in the Amish church anymore. But since God had revealed so many biblical truths, that are not practiced in the Amish church, I guess it's good that we are rejected.

I know all your cries are, "Make peace with the church!" But is it making peace with God when it's not biblical? We have to think what it would take to be right with the Amish church. We would have to confess that we did wrong by getting together to study God's Word and praying together. How could we do that? Yes, you would say, because they were not Amish people. Is that God's way? Does it not say it doesn't matter if you are Greek or Jew, circumcised or uncircumcised, etc. Also that God is no respecter of persons (Acts 10:34) and shows no partiality. Also someone asked Jesus once who is your brother. And He answered who ever does the will of the Father is your brother, sister, and mother. I could look it up but I'm sure you know what I'm talking about. It doesn't say whoever doesn't drive a car or dresses the same as you do. Whoever does His commandments and talks about the Lord Jesus. No, it does not specifically say that he who talks about Him also talks about exalting or glorifying His Name. How do we do that? It is just by doing good works? No, but also what is in the heart will come out of the mouth.

About those two verses you stated in 1 John 4:1 and 1 John 3:15. That is rightly so about not believing every spirit. We have to use discernment there. But the question is, "What is the world?" Anything that is not of God. We must remember when Jesus was talking of the world, it was before cars, telephones, TVs, and all such. But he was saying that some had world in them then already so what was it then? Do you think it was something that could be seen on the outside? It could have been. I'm not saying it wasn't but I think He was talking of the inward man — the carnal man. Anything that was not of God. In Romans 14:14 it says "that nothing is unclean in itself." It's what man makes unclean that is not right. Even the TV is not unclean in itself. If everything that came over it was godly and from the Bible it would be a good thing, but man has made it so corrupt so it's unclean most of the time. Almost scary, isn't it, as we always classed it such an evil thing.

Now to get on with some of the verses you quoted. In 1 Peter 2, we can't just pick out "a peculiar people" and go with that in our dress alone. We are peculiar to the world if we don't curse when something goes wrong, or try to get the best end in dealings or cheat etc., or go after the latest styles or try to show your figure with your dress [clothes]. Also, the Bible says to show forth the praises of Him ... are we doing that in our daily walk?

And in 1 Peter 2:13 you especially underlined to "submit to every ordinance of man." That surely does not mean the ordnung of the church like I think you are referring to, as it talks about a king or to governors. So it surely is talking about government. The New King James Bible lists as the title to the topic from verse 13 to 17, "Submission to Government."

For instance, the car is such a big issue. Is that not a commandment of men? If you really stop to think, even back in Jacob Amman's time [our Amish forefather], there were no cars at all. So we know that sometime along the line this became a commandment of man. If we think it is so wrong to own or drive one, why do we go in them at all? I'm sure we would all admit that we could hardly get along in life this day and age without using them at times. But remember God said there's nothing unclean in itself. I'm not saying it's wrong not to have one — that's up to the individual, but I guess what I'm saying is it is wrong when you count it as a sin, when you can nowhere in the Bible read something like that. You say, "Well, it's not Amish." Where are we putting our glory or trust? To Amish first, then God. Is that what the Bible teaches? Exodus 20:5 says, He is "a jealous God" and He wants "all the glory." ...

Oh, I feel so rude! Who am I to be saying all this to you? I guess we have gotten so many letters trying to tell us what to do out of their own philosophy and watch out this and watch out that. Hardly ever was the admonishment, "Search the Bible and see what it says" or "Trust in the Lord for Him to lead you." Your letter I think had actually the most Scripture in it. And now I am telling you, you are wrong in it. Oh, it just makes me cry to think of you reading this how hurt you will be. And my flesh would want to say, "Please don't let anyone see this letter," but I will give you permission to let anyone read this that you feel like sharing it with. As I feel I couldn't write everyone this much. I have so often just searched for something in the Bible to prove us wrong. I could never find that; instead, I learned more about God's plans and God's way.

Now I guess the last is the hardest part of all yet. Yes, Colossians 3:20 says, "Children, obey your parents" ... but surely that would mean too if it doesn't go against Scriptures. But too I think that's talking on the home [children at home yet]. "The Christian Home" is a title for verse 18 and on. It talks about the wives, then husbands and children and fathers, etc. But don't get me wrong that we don't want to heed to those other places where it says, "Honor thy father and mother." We do love them and have a concern for them and our desire would be to please them. But if they agree with and do things that we feel is not scriptural then how can we do everything they want us to?...

It makes me sad that Dad would say that we are not "walking in truth." As that is our greatest desire "to walk in the light and truth of His (God's) Word." God is real to us, and we want to completely trust in Him to lead us through this life and have no other gods before Jesus. We also realize more how alive and deceiving Satan is, but God still has power over him. In Ephesians 6 it talks about putting on the armor of God to stand against the wiles of the devil. For we do not wrestle against flesh and blood but against principalities and powers, against rulers of darkness (which is talking about Satan and his power), then it goes on the next five or six verses to tell us how to be prepared to fight against that power. I guess to best explain how we feel we were all these years is where in Matthew 15:8 – 9 it says, "These people draw near to Me with their mouth, and honor Me with their lips, but their heart is far from Me. And in vain they worship Me, teaching as doctrines the commandments of men."

I hope you don't think this is an easy thing to do, as it has been awfully hard and was not for our fleshly lusts either. Losing our two girls was not as hard as this. Sometimes when we were reading in the Bible and the Holy Spirit was revealing something to us, I just didn't want to go on reading for fear we'd get convicted of something else. I would rather have read something that would make me comfortable, like a Family Life story, or something that would hold up the Amish. It has been so hard to give up some of these things that were so dear to us, but we realize so much of it was our own righteousness and not the righteousness of God.

If anything is not biblical we would like to know. And we ask *anyone's prayers that read this that the Lord's will be done. Our prayer is that you all can "abound more and more" in the Word of God and trust in Him.*

Aus liebe,

Ora Jay and Irene

Circle Letter, Grieving Parents Group

October 28, 1998

Dear circling friends,

Greetings in Jesus' name from Montana! "Do not sorrow, for the joy of the LORD is your strength"(Nehemiah 8:10 NKJV). When we have that joy of the Lord, that is our strength even in difficult times. When things seem to be going good, when we don't have that joy, we will still be fretful or discontent.

I would like to get this letter going again. We (Ora Jay, baby, and I) were in Mexico last week and this came then so it's delayed a little bit. Seems it takes a half a week to get things going again after a trip. Yes, we went down to visit and be with Ora Jay's parents. His dad has cancer, so he went to the doctor in Mexico to treat his cancer. His mom had surgery too to repair her bladder; now she is not doing as well as his dad.

No. 3, wonder how your daughter's boyfriend is? God has a way of trying to get our attention and focus on Him in ways that are hard to understand. But He wants us to fully trust in Him in all circumstances. So many other incidents are accidents that Satan would like to use to destroy people, but he cannot do more than God allows him to do. And God can turn those attempts around for the good to those that love Him.

Oh, yes, we were blessed with another baby boy. Timothy Wayne. August 15. So he is two and a half months old now. He has been a good baby, but since we were in Mexico he has been more fussy. Wonder why? Must quit.

Ora Jay, Irene and all

Letter to Family

May 20, 1999

Dear family,

About your suggestion of making peace with the West Kootenai church. It would look almost impossible to us. There would be something we would have to give up which we feel would stunt our spiritual growth — like the prayer meetings, and the Bible studies that we have in our Sunday school classes. Plus we would have to compromise in quite a few things.

I think I can truly say that I love you all in a way that I haven't loved before. But I won't go into detail in this letter, but if anyone really wants to know what's in our hearts you can write us personally and we'll try to explain.

Ora Jay and Irene

CHAPTER 22

Complete Helplessness, Complete Hope

ORA JAY

August 1, 2010

Looking back we can see how our words — our good intentions — might have offended people. We were so transformed by what God had done in our lives that we wanted to share all we could. Soon, the circle letters stopped coming, and I knew that many people — other than our families — had dropped us from their lists. We talked too much about spiritual things. We were immature in a lot of ways, and we wanted everyone to change — now.

The years passed, the children grew and got married, and while we grew in our relationship with Christ, things haven't always been easy. More trials came, including one that left me completely helpless.

Before the day that changed everything I prided myself at being able to keep up with my boys. We worked together, logged together. I could run with them, sprint, jump ... and I loved being part of that. Then I got the stomach flu. I was still recovering when I went outside to the garden to pick some carrots. I brought them in, and by the time I got inside my hand was tingling. I rested a little bit downstairs on the couch, but then I could barely make it upstairs because of the weakness of my legs. It was a Thursday, and the next day I felt my legs weakening even more. Every time I went to the bathroom I grew weaker, to the point I could hardly walk. We headed to North Valley Hospital in Whitefish.

We arrived Friday evening after hours. They said I needed an MRI, but no one was around to do it. They told us to come back on Monday. By Saturday morning I couldn't get out of bed and couldn't walk. I tried and collapsed to the floor. We called our children and some of the church people. They gathered around me and prayed. Then I sat on a folding chair, and the boys carried me to the car. Wasn't it just last week I was running around with them, healthy and strong?

Irene had faith. "I don't know what's going on, but I sure don't feel it's a permanent thing," she told me.

We went back to the hospital. They sent us to the hospital in Kalispell where there were MRI techs on duty. The whole while I tried not to think of the cost. We had no insurance, but at that point it didn't matter. My body refused to move, and more than once I thought, "This may be my last day."

"God got us into this, He can surely get us out," Irene told me.

To both of us, it seemed like God was allowing this to happen. And even though I couldn't move, I could talk to God … and I did. The connection was strong.

Because of my condition I was immediately sent into intensive care, and it was discovered I had Guillain-Barré syndrome. Its causes are unknown, but it starts with a weakening of the limbs and moves to the trunk. Some people find themselves on a breathing and heart machine, but I didn't need that. I had a feeling the prayers of our family and friends had stopped its journey toward my heart.

In the hospital I couldn't feed myself. I couldn't even blow my nose. I lay there without moving as the hospital pumped $7,500 of medicine into me per day, over the course of five days. I talked to everyone I could about God. Not knowing if or when I would recover, I shared my faith and held nothing back. Some of the nurses and doctors prayed with me. Our kids stopped by, and our friends came, and I felt their concern. Our beautiful daughter, Saretta, a teen at this time, came with her guitar and sang to me. It was such a witness. God reminded me that though I'd lost friends He'd brought more. More than that, I knew Him — truly knew Him.

Our phone didn't stop ringing. So many wanted to know what they could do.

One person from back east called, and she hadn't even heard of my illness. She said, "I just want to know what's going on. You've come to our mind so often. Can we pray for you?"

When Irene told her, then she knew why she'd been praying.

Prayer chains went out — churches and people from all over prayed for me. Prayer was my strength. I'd been an Amish man who'd prided myself in all I could do, and now I could do nothing.

I was in the hospital bed for six weeks. Irene had to wash me and take me to the bathroom. Occupational therapists and physical therapists came to work with me, and God provided in so many ways. One day we got a $5,000 check from people whom we'd met briefly — who had come to Montana and stayed with us. What a blessing!

I went to the county fair just a few days after I was home in a battery-powered wheelchair. So many people wanted to stop and talk, and I shared what Jesus was doing with all of them.

But the most powerful experience was when my brother Daniel came to visit. He'd come for Gerald and Krista's wedding, and he helped me in so many ways. My fingers were so weak that I couldn't even unbutton my pants on my own. Yet he helped me and cared for me. And I needed him. I needed my brother.

The Lord used those weeks to help us bond with each other. Both of us came to a place of accepting each other for who we were. God had brought us together in a way that other things couldn't.

Since that time I have recovered much of my strength. It has been a slow process, but God is good. I can walk unassisted, but my gait is awkward. I don't have complete feeling in my legs. I don't have the strength in my arms that I used to have. Yet I have God, I have Irene, and I have my family. I've seen God bring me back from close to death, and my weakness reminds me to depend completely on His strength.

IRENE

Many years have passed since we found true hope in Christ. Our family still wishes and hopes that we'll return to the Amish. Just this last May we were at my father and stepmother's house. They let us sit at the table with them, for which we were thankful, but the disapproval was still evident in their gazes. Recently my sister, who herself had left the Amish for a time, rejoined an Amish community.

"Don't you think you can come back too?" *Dat* asked.

I told him I couldn't, and it broke his heart.

As we talked, we sat in a room that hasn't changed much since my growing-up years. While some Amish homes look similar to *Englisch* homes, except for the lack of electricity, my *dat's* home has remained fixed in time.

But it isn't the lack of conveniences that keeps me from wishing to return. Yes, I've gotten used to flipping on a switch for light and being able to travel more quickly by vehicle, but that isn't what keeps me away. I could give up those things easily if I had to. What I can't give up is the hope I've found in Jesus Christ. The hope Ora Jay and I have both found. Knowing that it's not what I do that puts me on God's good side, but the blood of Christ. I can never change His love for me. I don't want to forego my relationship based on love for one based on works.

God is a God who heals. We've seen His healing in our broken bodies, but even more on our broken hearts and minds. The closer we've drawn to God, the more we understand how man's laws had fractured our thinking. One cannot draw close to Jesus without discovering such healing. It makes me want to draw closer still ... and see what continued messages of hope He wishes to speak to our hearts.

"Ye have not, because ye ask not," God's Word says (James 4:2 KJV). And our prayer is that as you are nearly finished with our story of healing that you'll ask God to do a work in your heart. We are so blessed to be a part of what God has called us to do.

For so many years I strove to live the life of a godly woman, or at least that's what I would have told you. Instead, what I actually feared was people. I wanted to look good in their eyes. Even when we dedicated our lives to God's way, I missed out on the most important part. As the Bible says: "You study the Scriptures diligently because you think that in them you have eternal life. These are the very Scriptures that testify about me, yet you refuse to come to me to have life" (John 5:39–40).

But now I've found hope. Now I have found Jesus, and that's not something I can turn my back on. I'm thankful that God has opened the hearts of my husband and children. I'm thankful they have found Him too.

ORA JAY

We are the parents of nine children still on this earth, eight boys and one girl, ranging in ages from fifteen to thirty-five. And of course we have our two daughters in heaven. We've also been blessed with wonderful daughters-in-law and six grandchildren. Our daughters-in-law have blessed us with gifts beyond our expectations. They are good housekeepers and have hobbies such as quilt making, art and fashions, barrel racing, and more. They have great hearts for children and teach them manners, spend time with them, and love and appreciate them to a greater extent than we did. Also we are excited about our only daughter's upcoming marriage to a wonderful man who also has a heart for the Lord. So yes, we are very blessed!

Our daughter has blessed us with so many talents. She has touched many people with her beautiful voice, songwriting, guitar and piano playing. She has done charcoal drawings and paintings with her artistic talents, and with her great personality she has become a well-liked hair stylist. Yes, truly, she is a great blessing to us.

All of our children have chosen to accept Christ in their hearts and live for Him. When we left the Amish, the accusations came. People said, "You can't leave the Amish. Your family is going to fall apart. Your children will be wild, and you won't have any control over them. They're going to do all sorts of things you don't want them to." I'm thankful that has not been the case.

Over the years Irene and I have clung to Psalm 112:2: "Their children will be mighty in the land; the generation of the upright will be blessed." It doesn't say they may or could be blessed, but they *would* be. We hold that one personally. The testimony that we've had from the neighbors surrounding us is that they appreciate our children. This is a tremendous confirmation from the Lord.

We still live in Northwest Montana, and we still attend Kootenai Christian Fellowship. Our son Eli is the pastor there now, and Marion is the youth pastor. We are proud of all of our children.

We miss some things about being Amish, especially the family lifestyle that we always had together. Irene misses being with her sisters and getting together to help each other with their work — cleaning or canning or whatever. They'd always get together and help each other; that was a great community life.

The men did the same — the farmers especially. They'd get together and help each other out. The way they did things actually promoted that, because they couldn't do things by themselves. They'd have frolics to build a house or a barn. The frolics did not finish the whole structure, but the main work was done through the help of friends.

The Amish also make many unplanned visits, and this was a great joy to us. We'd be thrilled to see someone come up the road in a horse and buggy. We enjoyed it when someone stopped by to visit on the spur of the moment. This was common among the Amish. Visitors often stopped by unexpectedly, and they were always welcome.

These days, we don't have the same community connections. As a family we've gotten together for work days as our sons have built their own houses, and for bigger projects, but most of the time we need to plan and schedule even short visits. Today, most people aren't comfortable with someone coming into their house without warning. We all expect phone calls and appointments when people want to show up, rather than just knocking on the door and saying, "I'm here." The phone changes things.

I still believe, however, in the importance of our fellowship with each other as Christians. Scripture clearly tells us that we don't carry the full gift ourselves. We each have a gift, and we can see Jesus Christ expressing Himself through each other. It's God's design for us to be together as His children, to grow and to know Him more fully. Jesus said He only did what the Father was doing. We need to look to Jesus as the Author and Finisher of our faith (Hebrews 12:2). His Holy Spirit leads us into all truth (John 14:17). The Lord is close to all who call on Him; yes, to all who call on Him in truth (Psalm 145:18).

IRENE

We have kept some elements of our Amish life that we're thankful for. Ora Jay still drives horses, and we even have a business that provides wagon and carriage rides for special events. We also love serving people, and we have an open house policy.

We love to garden, raise chickens, and milk cows, and we know how to develop land into a dwelling place. We love doing 4-H with the rest of the community, and we find that the merchants and townspeople are very generous.

We were born Amish, but we were born-again into an eternal kingdom, and our most wonderful claim now is that we're children of the living God. We are saved by the blood of Jesus Christ, and grace has totally overwhelmed us. Jesus has totally brought us His freedom and His touch as we go through life.

ORA JAY

Irene and I came from a life that was supposedly simple — it looks simple and is promoted as being simple — but in truth it is hectic and busy. We spent a lot of time trying to please God, to earn our salvation by getting every little detail right — from dress to church to work. When we were living the Amish lifestyle, our hope was in what we did and what we got.

But now, as followers of Jesus, we know that we don't have to dress a certain way or reject technology to please Him. Yet even in our Christian walk at times "shoulds" and "expectations" creep in. *We should do this* or *We're expected to do that.*

Irene and I continually have to check our motives and our goals. Are we making a choice because that's what God is asking of us? Is this from the Lord? Or are we reverting back to what we know to do because of our background? Are our feelings reliable?

We came from an Amish background with a lot of securities that were not from the Lord. They were good things, good morals and beliefs, but anything that focuses our lives on works rather than God is an idol — even a good religious system.

People used to tell us, "Oh, you'll get to see your girls in heaven someday." But even as they said that there was an IF in the back of my mind. There was an IF in the back of their minds too. "Oh, you'll get to see your girls in heaven someday, IF you live a good enough life." Even as I tried to live the best life I could, I was never sure I was doing enough.

Irene has told me before that she'd wonder, "What if I died on a day when I committed a sin and I end up not being good enough?" I'm so thankful that we don't have to wonder anymore. Our faith is in Jesus Christ and in Him alone.

CHAPTER 23

Walking in Freedom

ORA JAY

I won't lie and say that I'm fine with how things are with our Amish family. I wish we had the close relationships we once had. More than that, my greatest hope is that they will discover the same freedom in Christ that we've found. The point isn't about being Amish or not being Amish; rather, it's realizing that you don't have to do any of those things to earn God's love, favor, or salvation. Trusting in Jesus is enough. It has always been enough.

Do you have a relationship with God? Do you know where you stand with God? And do you really believe?

Looking back, I'm amazed to see how God led us away from the Amish church. People often ask us about the moment we made the decision, but it wasn't like that. There wasn't one moment when we decided to leave. Instead, as we read God's Word, His sweet Holy Spirit would point out something that we hadn't seen before. We'd study the Scriptures and then study our lives, realizing how far we were from living in God's freedom. We could only handle a few truths at a time, and with God's help we did our best to change. We trusted God to bring about change in us as we sought Him. Unlike the Amish faith, which is made up of rules, these changes couldn't happen on their own.

We grew up Amish, thinking that we were elite. In fact, we heard preachers who said, "Only a few will get into heaven, but I guess there's not many Amish compared to the whole world," insinuating that mainly the Amish are going to go to heaven. Yes, some of the *Englisch* might get to heaven, but they probably didn't have a very good shot. We thought the *Englisch* must not have read the whole Bible to know what we knew.

We were talking with a friend just the other night, who told us that when she first left the Amish church, she started fellowshipping with other Christians. Once, when she was sitting in a circle with other believers, they started talking about the Bible. She felt silly because she realized she didn't know much about the Bible. Yet she was of the mind-set that she should know better than these non-Amish, because she'd been raised among better people. She didn't even know how to talk about Jesus and discuss the Bible in depth, because that's something the Amish just don't do.

What about you? Do you look to Jesus Christ (the life giver) who is life Himself through the Bible and let Him transform you? Or have you found yourself living the same way you were raised? Do you follow the traditions of man without fully understanding the grace of God?

We're telling our story now because the Lord has done so much for us, granting us His saving grace, peace, and rest. His love is so encouraging and satisfying. It doesn't matter if you've been Amish or Mormon or Baptist or whatever — Jesus Christ is the answer. The more that you can keep your eyes on the simple fact that He is your Savior and He lives in you, the better. Whatever we face today, we face with Jesus Christ, who walks with us daily.

IRENE

The hope I had to see my girls in heaven used to be a little bit foggy. Would I be good enough to make it? Now I have an assurance we will see them because of what the Bible says. If we are children of God, then we will inherit eternal life. It's a wonderful thing to know that we can surely just trust Jesus with our eternal life. In fact Jesus is eternal life, and we can live in it now!

My faith now is that I know Jesus loves me, whether I feel it or not. I know He forgives me, and that if I trust Him, He no longer sees my sins or shortcomings. He is such an awesome God. It's so different than always thinking, *Oh, now I should do more good, and if I do this just a little bit better I might be okay*. It's such a comforting thought to believe in His salvation. Following Him is not that hard. It's plain and simple.

I hope that after hearing our story you will see that only Jesus can get you to heaven, that a relationship with Him is all that you need. Accepting the fact that He is able to be in you, and that His Spirit is in you when you ask for the Holy Spirit to speak to you — well, it is enough. It has always been enough. Isn't it amazing that God shared His Son so that you can have a part of God Himself living in you!

Letter to Family

February 18, 2013

Dear Wilma,

Thank you for your letter and cards. We understand your great concern and where you are coming from. First of all we are grateful and very blessed with where we are. Geographically we are content and love living here because God brought us here. Spiritually we are constantly being touched by God and drawn closer to Him and know that He has so much more for us still. He has set us free and free indeed to serve God (as we die to self).

We did spend a lot of time studying, praying, searching history, etc. quite some time ago. (Before we made the decision about the head covering—this was not a quick one.) We just don't feel that the Amish life is what we want to practice. For us to try to explain to you would probably not change your mind, but one thing we would like to say to you—please find it in your heart not to be the judge of these trifling things, that don't change your heart and have nothing to do with your salvation....

Do you know who Jesus had the harshest words for? It was the people who were putting their emphasis on keeping the law rather than a relationship with Jesus. "But their hearts are far from me. Their worship of me is based on merely human rules they have been taught" (Isaiah 29:13). If we suppose that we can follow all the laws of the Bible and not miss one, but if we do (miss one) we might as well not do any. We will soon see that we are failing. Scripture says we are all born sinners and in need of a Savior. That is why Jesus came to set us free. Not to live by the letter of the law but by the Spirit. "For the letter kills, but the Spirit gives life" (2 Corinthians 3:6 NKJV).... You feel that your rules help you stay away from the world when the world is in the heart. Where the Bible talks about the world it's talking about a heart condition and not about any material things....

Every time I read the Love Chapter (1 Corinthians 13) it challenges me to love unconditionally, to love every size, shape, and color of people, whether they smell good or not, and even the ones we get irked at. We can do so many "good" things, but if we don't have love it does us no good. "Love never fails." Love is so important.

I'm sorry this has gotten quite lengthy but seems I'm not good at putting my thoughts down in a few words.

We know how we used to think, and it's possibly the way you are *thinking, that we are saying some of these things to try to cover up some of the things we are doing. But that is so far from the truth. The more we accept God's love for us, the more we see how great and awesome He is. That He is with us all the time when we surrender our life to Him. That there is nothing more important than having a relationship with Jesus and to live by His Spirit, and all things were made for Him and by Him.*

It is good to know that we can't do anything to earn our salvation. If we could, then it would not be a gift. It is by grace (something we don't deserve), through faith (in God alone), and it's not of yourselves; it is the gift of God, not by works (nothing done to earn it) so that no one can boast. It's by grace you have been saved (Ephesians 2:8 – 9).

We love you guys and your family. May the Lord keep drawing you closer to Himself.

Your sister,
Irene and Ora Jay

Acknowledgments

We are thankful for Tricia and John Goyer and family. We are thankful for their friendship and for Tricia's help in writing this story.

We are thankful for all the staff at Zondervan. Thank you for believing in us and God's work in our lives.

Thank you to all who have be a part of our lives — and our faith — as it has grown.

Finally we are thankful for our children — for their being part of this story. They journeyed with us toward Jesus. We are thankful that our lives were transformed together.